Stress-Less

In

5 Minutes

Tyra LaRocca

Copyright Notice

This publication is designed to provide accurate, authoritative and entertaining information in regard to the relief of stress symptoms or self-improvement. It is sold with the understanding that the publisher is not engaged in rendering legal, accounting, medical, or other professional services. If legal advice or other expert assistance is required, the services of a competent professional person should be sought.

Dedication

---

*To the very special people who bring joy and laughter
into my life, which makes all the stress meaningless...*

I am grateful.

Table of Contents

1. What Stress???

It's Monday. You've started out behind, overslept, couldn't find the right clothes for the days' obligations, and run right into backed-up traffic. Uggh!

That's not *Stress*, that's just *LIFE*, right? Well, yes it is, and it can just be a normal part of life depending on how you and your body handle it. Let's look for a moment at what stress is, and what it can do to you and your health. This is the background, educational section, so if you feel like you have stress figured out, just skip to the next section where all the actual stress solutions are found.

Stress is a normal physical response to a situation which makes you feel threatened or upset. When threatened, it triggers the Fight (combat the cause of the stress), Flight (actively avoid dealing with it), or Freeze (do nothing) response. You then choose one of these three options to deal with the situation. Most people have a tendency to use one way of handling stressful situations more often than the other two.

When your body perceives a threat, your Central Nervous System kicks into action, releasing a multitude of stress hormones that prepare your body for action. These physical changes help you to focus your mind, energize you and keep you alert and ready for whatever comes next.

These are the times when a 120 pound mom lifts the front of a car because her child is stuck underneath it. Or when you get that prickly sensation on the back of your neck and suddenly you know you need to move away.

These are natural reactions to very real dangers.

The stress we will be dealing with in these activities is more of the day-to-day, sometimes overwhelming, but generally not dangerous type. You know, *LIFE*.

~Stress-Less in 5 Minutes~

Like most anything needing change, the first step is awareness. You need to know when you are stressing and how this manifests in your body. Perhaps you just thought the reason you snapped at your spouse or coworker was that you didn't get enough sleep. What if you didn't get enough sleep because your mind is on overload from all the worries and commitments knocking around in your head at night? Then, the lack of sleep, which is a symptom of your stress, makes you more likely to have a short fuse (also a symptom), and you snap more easily at others.

How do you know if it's stress or lack of sleep? Great question!

One simple way to determine this is to look at a list of common, but by no means exhaustive, symptoms of stress and mark any and all that you currently experience (which you know don't apply to another physical/emotional issue you may have, like Irritable Bowel Syndrome or Congestive Heart Failure, to name a couple).

Check, circle or write down the ones below which apply to you now.

Stress Symptoms

Fatigue

Low energy

Insomnia

Headache

Body aches

Tension

Chest pain/tightness

Fast Heartbeat

Diarrhea

~What Stress???~

Difficulty Concentrating

Constipation

Nausea

Heartburn

Difficulty Breathing

Frequent Colds/Illness

Rashes, Itching, Hives

Loss of Sexual Desire/Ability

Stuttering

Gritting or Grinding Teeth

Forgetful, Absent-minded

Light headed- Dizzy

Dry Mouth

Feeling Overwhelmed

No interest in Appearance

Increase in Minor Accidents

Overreacting to Minor Things

Sudden Panic Attacks

Frequent Sighing

Cold or Sweaty Palms

Reduced Productivity

Trouble Learning New Things

Frequent Crying Spells

Gambling or Impulse Purchases

Increased Irritability, Edginess

Lying or Making Excuses to Cover up Problems

Withdrawing from Social Situations

Increased/Decreased Appetite/Weight

Increased Use of over-the-counter drugs

Increased Smoking, Alcohol or Drug use

Now, add up your checked items. How did you fare?

If you have less than 3, you probably are not currently feeling terribly stressed. You may not be completely relaxed, but chances are you aren't feeling these symptoms all the time. Good for You!

If you checked 5 or more, chances are your body has been feeling the effects of worry and anxiety for at least a few days now. Take the time to work on these in the next sections. Be sure to keep track of how you feel every day until they subside.

If you checked 10 or more, you certainly may now, or in the future, have some unwelcome physical and emotional ailments coming your way. Stress increases risk factors for almost any major medical problem, from ulcers to heart disease. The key is to find ways to cope with stress more effectively. You may also want to check with your doctor to rule out any serious or chronic conditions, just to be safe.

First, you'll be taking your temperature, so to speak, to see where you are with your stress level. You will do well to check how you feel stress-wise every day.

Then, we'll be looking at simple ways you can better tolerate your daily stress, and even reduce it, quickly and easily. Sound good?

Let's do it!

How to Use This Guide

This book has been arranged for you to find quick activities that you can do to quash the stress effects you're experiencing based on the amount of time you have, and where you are located when you do them.

Keep in mind that many of the suggested stress-busting strategies can be done in many places, so there will be multiple listings for some, and you can bookmark the ones you find most helpful for you.

Before you start any stress reducing option, rate your current stress level. Ask yourself to rate your stress on a scale of 1 to 10, with 1 being stress-free to 10 signifying the most stress you've ever felt (May also be a good time to check in with your doctor).

After you complete an activity, re-rate your stress level on the same 1-10 scale. If you haven't found sufficient relief, you may want to do some Deep Breathing, check your 1-10 level again, and follow up with another exercise if you still feel the need. It may be unrealistic to bring your level from an 8 to a 2 in only 5 minutes, but you will know at what level you can perform your necessary tasks competently. A good first result is finding your stress number go down by at least 2 points.

Now you're ready to de-stress. Here's how:

~Stress-Less in 5 Minutes~

Pick your time frame first:

Do you only have a quick 5 minutes to diffuse the tension, unclench the muscles and relax? Go to the Section, *When You Have 5 Minutes*. If you have up to 30 minutes, go to the *When You Have 30 Minutes* section. And if you have an hour or more start with the section *When You Have 1+ Hour*.

Then Pick your location:

Start first with the section that matches where you are when you want to de-stress: *Home, Work, or Outside*. Also check out activities in the other sections if your location is flexible.

Pick one or more activities. Try one, and if you don't get as much relief as you'd like, repeat the activity or try another one.

Sometimes, depending on the type of stress you are feeling, or where in your body you are feeling it, you may need to experiment to find out whether *Deep Breathing* is enough to calm you and allow you to keep working or dealing with your present circumstance.

If *Deep Breathing* isn't enough, do you need to restart by taking a Cat Nap, or a Walk Outside? If your body is especially tense, Stretching, Massage or Acupressure may do the trick quickly.

You will see this dollar sign to note activities that may cost you money.

$ - Cost may be involved

Some stress-busters may appear in more than one list, can be used in more than one place, or for longer/shorter periods of time. You may come to have your own favorite go-to stress-busters over time. I do, too, but I would highly recommend trying as many of them as makes sense for you to have a myriad of options at your disposal, no matter where you are when you feel stressed.

Ready? Let's get you feeling better!

2. When You Have 5 Minutes

When you feel the anxiety creeping into your shoulders, neck or belly, sometimes taking five minutes to relax can fend it off. Five minutes might not seem like much time, and it may not be, but if you act quickly it can mean the difference between falling down the stress cycle like a snowball multiplying as it rolls down a hill, or returning to a peaceful, more relaxed state.

5 Minutes At Home

Choose one or more of these easy, fast stress-busting activities to get you back to normal awesomeness in a flash. Even in your PJ's.

Deep Breathing

Typically my first go-to calming activity is deep breathing. If you already do this when you get angry or nervous, or when you meditate or do yoga, you know how calming it can be. And what could be easier? You can do it anywhere.

Sitting or lying down are both great options to do this exercise, Sit or lie down in a comfortable place, feet on the floor (or stretched out straight), arms relaxed at your sides or in your lap. If you can close your eyes it will help shut out the distractions.

~Stress-Less in 5 Minutes~

Take a deep breath in slowly through your nose as you count to five. Hold for a few counts, and then slowly exhale through your mouth for a count of five. As you inhale, you can say to yourself (in your head) any word or phrase which will calm you. Examples: Calm, Relax, In with Calm, Peace, I'm relaxing now, and so on.

As you exhale, say to yourself one of these or a similar phrase: Letting Go, Stress is leaving, Relaxed, Out with pain/stress/anxiety.

Repeat the inhale/exhale process at least 10 times and you should start to feel more relaxed. A plus is that deep breathing like this also lowers your blood pressure and delivers more oxygen to your body which helps you be healthier in a variety of ways. Take a blood pressure reading before and after to see if it's true for you!

Probably best NOT to do this while driving, especially with your eyes closed!

Cup of Tea

Part of the reason a cup of tea is relaxing is the ritual involved in making and serving tea. While you may not have the time or inclination to serve tea as it is done in a ceremony in Japan or China (check out online videos about the tea ceremony, they're amazing, and relaxing in themselves), you can use the time preparing it to slow down and focus on brewing the tea to just the right strength and temperature for you.

Another perk for having a cup of tea is that you can find a flavor of tea with herbs for almost any ailment. If you stock up on the herbal blends which will most likely help you, the 5 minute cup of tea is simple. Here are some common teas for stress:

- Passionflower

- Ashwagandha

- Siberian Ginseng

- Hawthorne

- Chamomile

These ingredients can be found in many herbal teas, or you can find online recipes to brew your own. Follow the recommended water temperature and steeping time for the best flavor. Enjoy, and relax!

Take a Shower

Water is calming for most people. Remember the commercial for Calgon bath bubbles? *Calgon, take me away...ahh.* It's true, and in 5 minutes you can't really enjoy the bubble bath option, but a warm, soothing shower (or a cold one to wake you up and invigorate your body) can cleanse away the stress and leave you feeling new and relaxed. Add music or ambience as you like.

Massage Your Head

There are a variety of options with this one. If you want to have some massage implements at the ready, here are a few to choose from. You may have seen the wiry octopus-looking head massager and thought it was too ridiculous to be effective. Well, for a great many people who have tried or swear by them, you'd be wrong. Yes, it looks weird, but using one in the privacy of your own home will have you reaching for it even before you get a headache as it provides lots of tingly, soothing and relaxing sensations. Find your favorite option easily at your favorite online or jumbo in-store retailer. Buy multiples and keep one in your car, office, and a few hiding places, as they are sure to be 'borrowed' by others who try them.

Another popular and effective head/neck/shoulder massage tool is using essential oils to massage away the pain and tension. There are some great already formulated oils at retailers or health stores which target head and neck tension. Usually they will be named for the specific ailment. You can also make your own. The top essential oils for headaches/muscle tension are:

- Eucalyptus

- Spearmint

- Peppermint

- Chamomile

- Lavender

You can make your own massage oils by using one or more of the above essentials with a carrier oil like jojoba, sunflower or sweet almond oil. Here are a few recipes, find more online.

- Combine 1 oz. Carrier oil with 8 drops of Lavender and 4 drops of Peppermint oils in a dark glass bottle/jar with stopper or dropper
- Combine 1 oz. Carrier oil with 4 drops of Eucalyptus and 4 drops of Spearmint oil, in a glass bottle/jar.
- Combine 1 oz. Carrier oil with 8 drops of Lavender and 4 drops of Chamomile oil, in a glass bottle/jar.

Gently mix the ingredients.

Whether you purchase a targeted infusion or make your own, the important step is to take 3-4 drops of the oil on your fingertips and slowly massage into your temples, forehead, behind your ears and into the top of your neck. If you have someone else who can do this for you, even better, you can close your eyes and relax. Don't forget to put your fingers under your nose and breathe in the fragrance, it is also great for clearing your sinuses. Be careful to wash your hands afterward to avoid accidently getting the oils in your eyes.

In a pinch, if you don't have any of these tools, you can still massage the same spots with your fingers and any lotion, but the aromas above will be much more effective. Carry a small bottle in your purse, or car to have handy.

This is even better if you have someone else do the massage for you...

Smile in the Mirror

Did reading the heading make you want to smile, a little? Even the suggestion can be enough to break the tension. Have you ever been in a heated discussion, or a scary moment and you or someone else said something funny, lightening the mood? Yep, research supports that it doesn't take much to change your mood; your body actually prefers to be positive and happy. So when you don't have much time, find a mirror and look into your eyes and smile. Make faces if you like. Hold a smile for 60 seconds and your body thinks you must be enjoying yourself.

And you will be. ;)

Hug a Pet or Person

There are numerous studies which show the healing and calming effect a pet can have on you. They love attention, and love giving it to you. I have a cat who instinctively knows when I am upset, and she will talk to me, rub against me and not leave me alone until I'm laughing at her, assuring her that I'm OK. Make a point of spending a few minutes with your favorite furry friend, and you'll feel loved, and much calmer. If you don't have a pet (I'd suggest getting one...) visit one, or find a person you know well enough to give you a big hug. There are also substantial research findings showing that we humans need a minimum of 6 or more hugs a day for optimal health. Have you met your quota today?

Sending you a hug...

Acupressure

You may not know much about the ancient healing properties of Acupressure, but you will certainly be grateful to know a few pressure points on your body which when pressure is applied, will give you nearly immediate relief from stress. Here are a couple to try, and you will always have them with you, no matter where or when you need them.

- Look at your left palm, and take three fingers from your right hand, place them horizontally starting at the middle of the crease where your wrist and arm meet. At three fingers width, in the center is the acupressure point called the *Inner Gate*. Take your thumb and apply firm, but not painful pressure to this spot for 2 minutes. Switch to the other arm and repeat. This point is also great for relieving nausea.
- Another easy to find stress-relieving acupressure point is known as the *Sea of Tranquility*. You will find it in the center of your breastbone, in the indent or hollow of your sternum. Apply firm pressure here for 2 or more minutes and feel the wave of calm. Combine this with some deep breathing to ensure fast relief.

There are acupressure points for many more ailments, so you might want to research some of them for your own particular health needs.

Search Furniture for Hidden Money

Who doesn't love finding lost money? The promise of treasure makes the search exciting. Of course, in my couch there may also be other, less spendable objects. Assorted pens, potato chips and hair ties, mostly. You may find some items that make you smile, finding the answer to "Where did that (insert thing here) go?" And of course the most sought after change, bills or even credit cards. My biggest cache was $5.33. Not a lot, you're thinking, but I felt suddenly rich, and much less stressed. Try it.

Watch a Funny Video

This one is so easy, but beware, even though it's listed under the 5 minute section, once you get started, you may lose track of time and be watching videos until the kids, pets or the bathroom forces you to stop! Some of my favorites involve talking dogs, cat antics and laughing babies. Finding your own favorites is as easy as going to youtube.com or doing a search for funny videos.

You might want to set a timer.

Scream into a Pillow

Did you ever do this as a kid, so as not to wake others? I did. When the frustration level was so high that I wanted to, well scream, I would lie on my bed, face buried in my pillow and let it out. The release of pent up emotion can be a phenomenal thing, like a balloon when you let go of the end and the release of air sends it flying around. You're never too old to clear out the anxiety and anger that can build up inside. You may want to make sure nobody else is around, but chances are you won't need the entire 5 minutes to get rid of the stress and start feeling free again. Beware, if you're anything like me, you may end up with a hoarse throat, so you may want to fill the remainder of your 5 minutes with the Glass of Wine remedy...

Punch a Pillow

This is quite similar to the Scream into a Pillow option above, but much gentler on your vocal chords and you don't need to worry as much about waking others. It can feel just as relaxing, and much better for your hands than a wall or other similar hard surface. Punch away to your heart's desire.

Bonus-it's also great exercise!

Enjoy a Piece of Chocolate

Chocolate is definitely a comfort food for many people, and for me one of my top 2 food groups. When you are stressed you may not think that you could stop at one piece. However, if you have some decadent dark chocolate or a favorite truffle handy (who doesn't?), I challenge you to eat it very slowly, close your eyes, and savor the flavor, texture, aroma, and the feeling it brings. When consciously consumed, you will get more of the benefit of its indulgent quality. And, as a plus, much like wine, it has some fantastic health benefits.

Yum…

Have a Glass of Wine

Yes, it can help you relax, and also provide some heart-healthy benefits. Choose your favorite, and find a comfy spot to enjoy. Pair with some fruit or cheese and pretend you're at a café in Rome or Paris…

Even if it is only 10 a.m., you know it's 5 o'clock somewhere!

Salute!

Sing Your Favorite Song

It doesn't matter if you think you sound like the top-selling vocalist of all time, or have the best shower voice bar none; anyone can and should sing. Pick one of your favorite sing-a-longs and just let go, with or without music. Don't be shy, put your heart into it, play air guitar, dance like nobody's watching…

Then, hear the roar of your fans…

Doesn't it feel awesome to be you?

Dance

Like the *Sing Your Favorite Song* strategy above, this one requires that you let go, pretend that nobody is watching, and dance your little heart out. Pop on your favorite music, and be the best ballerina, hip-hop or break dancer anyone has ever seen. You will feel energized and freed, if only for 5 minutes. Carry the joyful feeling with you, or keep it going and do as my daughter suggests, *dance with your head* while doing other things.

You sure are light on your feet.

Stretch

When your muscles get so tense that they start sending you de-stress signals, one first line of defense is to stretch them out. Work out some of the lactic acid build-up and they will move more freely. If you have just a couple places you feel the stress, work specifically on those.

Yoga poses are amazing for stretching gently, and one overall fantastic stretching pose is a dead man pose. Lie on the floor on your back, legs and arms straight. Just relax each part of your body into the floor, muscle by muscle. Start at your feet and deliberately relax your feet, then your calves, thighs, and so on up to your head. As you pay attention to each part, you will feel the release, until you just melt into the floor.

If you can't lie on the floor, another way to stretch your body is to stand with your feet shoulder width apart, and bend over at the waist until you feel the stretch in your back and legs. Let your head and arms dangle. Hold this and breathe deeply. As you relax and your muscles unkink, you will sink lower to the ground. Hold as long as comfortable. Do this periodically throughout the day as you start to feel tense.

Bonus, if you stretch every night before bed, you'll be rewarded in the morning with less stiffness in your body!

Spray Some Lavender Mist

Similar to the massage oil found in the *Massage Your Head* section, an essential oil mist can be very calming, and Lavender is one of the most calming scents out there. Spray a room, or your pillow, sheets or your shirt to breathe in the marvelous lavender scent and feel its soothing, calming benefits quickly. Find it at home and body stores, or online. Keep it handy, my kids used to have a bottle in their bedroom and would spray their pillows when they had trouble sleeping.

Light a Lavender or Ocean Scented Candle

Much like the Mist idea above, lighting a stress-busting scented candle can encourage you to relax and slow down. Lavender, Chamomile, and Ocean scents are great choices, but if you have other ones that remind you of a happy, stress-free time, those will also work.

Just don't get so comfy that you fall asleep with it burning!

Blow Bubbles

This strategy is to help you have some fun, and feel like a kid again without a care in the world. Have a bottle of old-fashioned bubbles handy, and take the wand out, blow or swing and have some fun. Try to catch them, without breaking the bubble! If you have any children nearby, invite them to join you. You'll feel the tension drain away, and sport a great big smile.

Let out your inner child!

Schedule Another 5 Minutes...

If you've tried one of these 5 minute strategies, and still feel stressed, try another one, or do one a second time, as long as time allows. A great pre-emptive strategy is to plan to do a 5 minute tension-zapper every hour or two to ensure you feel your best.

What do you have to lose? (Perhaps a bunch of Stress?)

5 Minutes At Work

Choose one or more of these tips to de-stress without injury or bother to workmates.

Deep Breathing

Typically my first go-to calming activity is deep breathing. If you already do this when you get angry or nervous, or when you meditate or do yoga, you know how calming it can be. And what could be easier? You can do it anywhere.

Sitting is the best option for work, so start by sitting comfortably, feet on the floor, arms relaxed at your sides or in your lap. If you can close your eyes it will help shut out the work reminders.

Take a deep breath in slowly through your nose as you count to five. Hold for a few counts, and then slowly exhale through your mouth for a count of five. As you inhale, you can say to yourself (in your head) any word or phrase which will calm you. Examples: Calm, Relax, In with Calm, Peace, I'm relaxing now, and so on.

As you exhale, say to yourself one of these or a similar phrase: Letting Go, Stress is leaving, Relaxed, Out with pain/stress/anxiety.

Repeat the inhale/exhale process at least 10 times and you should start to feel more relaxed. A plus is that deep breathing like this also lowers your blood pressure and delivers more oxygen to your body which helps you be healthier in a variety of ways.

Probably best NOT to do this while driving, especially with your eyes closed!

Learn a Joke

Are you an accomplished joke-teller? I am not. I frequently forget the punchline, and even my own name some days! Whether you are or aren't proficient at getting a laugh from someone else, it can be a fun and ultimately rewarding skill to acquire. Perhaps you heard a joke that you enjoyed, and feel uncomfortable sharing it for fear of botching the presentation (or the punchline...). Or you want to add something new to the worn out jokes that most of your family and friends have heard (ad infinitum). Either way, learning a new joke will require some concentration, and practice- preferably in front of a mirror. Taking your concentration off something frustrating and finding a new, more interesting task can alleviate the worry you were experiencing.

There are numerous websites that have lists of jokes, or you can watch some videos for ideas. Be sure to mention the comedian if you share one of his/her jokes. Even if you never tell the joke to another soul, you can still feel gratified that if the need arises and nobody else can break the tension, you can be the hero.

Go you! (*Clapping*)

Tell a Joke

This technique skips the learning of the joke process (you've already GOT this), and goes straight to sharing it with someone else. When you make someone else smile, laugh or at least chuckle, you will feel better. Polish up your best one(s) for the circumstance and share robustly, even if only with the cat. Here's mine, a blonde joke (and I'm a blonde):

A blonde walks into a bank in New York City, says she's going to Europe for 2 weeks, and needs to borrow $5,000.

The bank officer says they'll need some kind of collateral, and she hands them the keys to a brand-new Rolls Royce parked in front of the bank.

The bank president and others enjoy a good laugh at the blonde for using a $250,000 Rolls as collateral for a $5,000 loan. A bank employee then drives the Rolls into the bank's underground garage.

Two weeks later, the blonde returns, repays the $5,000 and the interest, which is $25.41. The loan officer says "Miss, we are happy to have your business, but we're a little puzzled. We checked you out, and you're a multi-millionaire. Why would you bother to borrow $5,000?

The blonde replies, "Where else in New York City can I park my car for two weeks for only $25.41 and expect it to be there when I return?

Not what you expected, was it? Top that.

Cup of Tea

Part of the reason a cup of tea is relaxing is the ritual involved in making and serving tea. While you may not have the time or inclination to serve tea as it is done in a ceremony in Japan or China (check out videos online, relaxing in itself), you can use the time preparing it to slow down and focus on brewing the tea to just the right strength and temperature for you.

Another perk for having a cup of tea is that you can find a flavor of tea with herbs for almost any ailment. If you stock up on the herbal blends which will most likely help you, the 5 minute cup of tea is simple. Here are some common teas for stress:

- Passionflower

- Ashwagandha

- Siberian Ginseng

- Hawthorne

- Chamomile

These ingredients can be found in many herbal teas, or you can find recipes to brew your own online. Follow the recommended water temperature and steeping time for the best flavor.

Enjoy, and relax!

Let Go

Sometimes, do you just feel like you have the weight of the entire world resting on your sagging, painful shoulders? Most likely the vast majority of the issues you are carrying around aren't even yours. You may worry that your child passes his math test, or it doesn't rain for your outdoor party this weekend, and so on. Do you really have control over these, and many other things? No. So why let the worry of all the what-if's related to them bring you down?

You don't have to let it continue. You can let some (or all) of it go. If this scares you, then you definitely need to try it.

My favorite is taken from the Sedona Method, (Sedona.com) which is worth learning more about. It's an easy process, just three steps involved. First think about the thing that you are concerned/worried about- let's say you're worried that you'll make it to an important meeting on time. Fill in the thought with your particular concern.

1. OK, think to yourself, *This worry about getting to the meeting on time, COULD I let it go? Just could I?* Don't answer yourself, just let the thought sink in.

2. Now ask yourself, *This worry, Would I be WILLING to let it go?* See how that feels. If you feel like the answer is NO, ask, *Would I rather have this feeling or be free?*

3. Next ask yourself simply, *WHEN?* After you go through this 3 step process, check back and see how you feel about the issue. Chances are it's much less worrisome or urgent for you now. You can also repeat the process 2 or more times until the level of stress is much lessened.

Doesn't it feel great? You can do this anywhere, any time. And now you look taller!

Smile at Someone

For no reason at all, and without expectation of a returned smile, walk around and just flash your pearly whites to someone. If you can't go anywhere, find a mirror (or keep one in your desk) and smile ridiculously at yourself. It might seem insincere at first, funny even. That's OK. If you plan to complete 5 minutes of smile therapy, know that in addition to your body being tricked into thinking you are deliriously happy, you never know who else just had their day made from your small gesture.

Pretty (or handsome) sweet!

Plug in to Your Music

Ahh, music. Soothes both the savage beast and frayed nerves. Many people are able to work with music playing, but if you're not, why not plug yourself in to some that helps you relax- for just a few minutes?

Have a playlist just for this purpose. Put together some calming instrumentals or inspiring ballads that slow down the thoughts in your head. I like to pick a radio station on iHeart Radio or Pandora for Coffeehouse or Spa music. Have it ready and you'll be feeling more zen in no time.

Walk Around

Sometimes a simple change of location can break a cycle of stress. If you can, walk away from your desk or office and keep moving for a few minutes. Get the blood pumping, which will get your body to use the energy you're bottling up for something better than stress. If you can walk outside, even better. Try to ignore everything around you and just concentrate on moving. This is a great activity to do every hour or so as preventive medicine for stress. And at the end of an eight hour day, you'll have spent *35 or more minutes exercising!*

Who needs a gym?

Say Thank You

Gratitude is one of the best habits you can cultivate. It is a cure for so many things, and a magnet for all the things you appreciate. At work, it may seem as though thank you is not in the corporate vernacular. This certainly doesn't mean that people won't appreciate being thanked for what they do-even if it is their job. So, how about saying thank you to someone whose work you appreciate.

You can start with yourself! You deserve it, too. Move on to at least one other person and thank them in person or email. When you do this, the other person feels validated for their efforts, and will most likely feel inspired to help you again. There's that magnet working, bringing you more of that for which you are thankful. And you feel better.

Start a new daily habit. Say Thanks!

Acupressure

You may not know much about the ancient healing properties of Acupressure, but you will certainly be grateful to know a few pressure points on your body which when pressure is applied, will give you nearly immediate relief from pain or stress. Here are a couple to try, and you will always have them with you, no matter where or when you need them.

- Look at your left palm, and take three fingers from your right hand, place them horizontally starting at the middle of the crease where your wrist and arm meet. At three fingers width, in the center is the acupressure point called the *Inner Gate*. Take your thumb and apply firm, but not painful pressure to this spot for 2 minutes. Switch to the other arm and repeat. This point is also great for relieving nausea.

- Another easy to find stress-relieving acupressure point is known as the *Sea of Tranquility*. You will find it in the center of your breastbone, in the indent or hollow of your sternum. Apply firm pressure here for 2 or more minutes and feel a slow wave of calm flow over you. Combine this with some deep breathing to assure fast relief.

There are acupressure points for many more ailments, you might want to research some of them for your own particular health needs.

Massage Head/Shoulders

There are a variety of options with this one. If you want to have some massage implements at the ready, here are a few to choose from.

You may have seen the wiry octopus-looking head massager on late night TV and thought it was too ridiculous to be effective. Well, for a great many people who have tried or swear by them, you'd be wrong. Yes, it looks weird, but using one in the privacy of your own home will have you pulling it out even before you get a headache as it provides lots of tingly, soothing and relaxing sensations. Find your favorite easily at your favorite online or jumbo in-store retailer. Buy multiples and keep one in your car, office, other hiding places, as they are sure to be coveted by others who try them.

Another popular and effective head/neck/shoulder massage tool is using essential oils to massage away the pain and tension. There are some great formulated oils at retailers or health stores which target head and neck tension. Usually they will be named for the specific ailment. You can also make your own. The top essential oils for headaches/muscle tension are:

- Eucalyptus

- Spearmint

- Peppermint

- Chamomile

- Lavender

You can make your own massage oils by using one or more of the above essentials with a carrier oil like jojoba, sunflower or sweet almond oil. Here are a few recipes, find more online.

- Combine 1 oz. Carrier oil with 8 drops of Lavender and 4 drops of Peppermint oils in a dark glass bottle/jar with stopper or dropper
- Combine 1 oz. Carrier oil with 4 drops of Eucalyptus and 4 drops of Spearmint oil, in a glass bottle/jar.
- Combine 1 oz. Carrier oil with 8 drops of Lavender and 4 drops of Chamomile oil, in a glass bottle/jar.

Gently mix the ingredients.

Whether you purchase a targeted infusion or make your own, the important step is to take 3-4 drops of the oil on your fingertips and slowly massage the oil into your temples, forehead, behind your ears and into the back of your neck. If you have someone else who can do this for you, even better, you can close your eyes and relax. Don't forget to put your fingers under your nose and breathe in the fragrance, it is also great for clearing your sinuses. Be careful not to get any of the oil in your eyes as it's very strong and irritating for eyes.

In a pinch, if you don't have any of these tools, you can still massage the same spots with your fingers and any lotion, but the herbs above and their aromas will be much more effective.

Watch a Funny Video

This one is so easy, but beware, even though it's listed under the 5 minute section, once you get started, you may lose track of time and be watching videos until the kids, pets or the bathroom forces you to stop! Some of my favorites involve talking dogs, cat antics and laughing babies. Finding your own favorites is as easy as going to youtube.com or doing a search for funny videos.

You may want to set a timer.

Look Out a Window

Everyone knows that offices with windows are coveted. It makes sense since having a view to the outside, or even just natural light can lift your spirits. If you are fortunate enough to have a window nearby, don't forget to look out every once in a while. What you see may help your mind wander from your daily grind, and may even provide you inspiration to complete or solve a current work challenge.

If you don't have a window in your office space, go to where there is one. Just look out, scan the panorama and put yourself out there in it for a few minutes. Escaping for a short time to another place can be freeing, and you may be surprised at the insight available if you open your mind to the experience. At a minimum, you will feel like you had a break, and are not completely stuck in the office.

Enjoy the view!

Repeat a Mantra

A mantra is a sound, word or phrase that is repeated over and over to aid in concentration or meditation. It is originally a Buddhist or Hindu concept, but has traveled across the globe and found some additional uses. You may have used one for meditation to focus your mind, such as *Om*, or any word like *focus* or *breathe*.

Repeated while breathing deeply can help to pinpoint your focus on the word. It may also be used like a slogan, to identify with a sports team or company. For realtors, one mantra is *Location, location, location*. Your company may have one that you could use. Or, you could choose a word or phrase which signifies what you want to achieve or have. Possible words might be *peace, relaxed, inspired*, or anything that feels right to you.

You can repeat the mantra in your mind if you don't have privacy, but it is better if you can stop, close your eyes and say it out loud slowly, concentrating on its meaning and bringing it to you right now. Just be sure not to use a word that adds to the stress, such as deadline, losing, or stress!

You can carry your mantra with you, and use it whenever you like.

...Feeling rejuvenated...

Delegate

This is one of my favorite activities (and mantras). Do you absolutely, positively need to do everything? Or could you get some help? Especially if you are on a tight deadline, it might be just what the doctor ordered to give some of the responsibilities to someone who is good at what you need. When you do, the other person will feel good for helping (assuming they agreed to help), you will have less stress, and you can then shower your colleague with gratitude. And as we learned in an earlier stress-less activity, what you are thankful for brings you more of it. It's a win-win-future win!

You don't have to be super-worker, you can have a sidekick.

So go, share the fun.

Splash Water on Your Face

If your problem involves severe lethargy or a desperate need for a nap, and you just can't do that now, this can be a mini-wake up. Go to the restroom, take a good look in the mirror to assess your stress/tired level, and then prepare yourself to splash away at your face.

Put your hair back, take off your glasses, cover your shirt, tie or whatever may not enjoy contact with water, and splash or dab your face, preferably with cool water. Take care not to mess up any makeup, unless you brought your fixing supplies. Do this a few times until you feel the skin tingle awake. Pretend you are someplace exotic and want to rinse and relax at this beautiful stream.

Take a minute or more to just feel the wake-up call of the water, and then dry off, put yourself back together and carry on.

Savor a Piece of Chocolate

Chocolate is definitely a comfort food for many people, and for me one of my top 2 favorite food groups. When you are stressed you may not think that you could stop indulging at only one piece. However, if you have some decadent dark chocolate or a favorite truffle handy (who doesn't?), I challenge you to eat one piece very slowly, savoring the flavor, texture, aroma, and the feeling it brings. When consciously consumed, you will get more of the benefit of its indulgent quality. And, as a plus, much like wine, it has some fantastic health benefits.

Hmm...double win.

Straighten Your Desk/Space

Sometimes clearing a space can also clear your mind. If you are surrounded by chaos, you may not even realize that it has an impact on how you're feeling and how you concentrate (or don't) while in the space. If you are constantly looking through piles and stacks of papers and files, you waste valuable time, and your body will react to the untidy and unproductive space.

You may not notice, but try cleaning up a space, perhaps the top of your desk as a start, and see how you feel afterward. Just looking at the cleared space may make you feel so much better. In fact, if you feel like your space is hopelessly messy, I challenge you to make a point of picking an area each day or week to organize until it feels better. You must then keep up with it for the good feelings to continue, unlike my kids who would often take days to clean their room, only to allow the piles to accumulate almost immediately.

If you don't know where or how to start, enlist the help of the office organizer. Don't not do it because you don't think you can. It will pay off, in less stress, and higher productivity.

What do you have to (find) lose?

Pop Some Bubble-Wrap

Who doesn't love popping some bubble-wrap? Even my cat loves to play with it, and freaks out every time she breaks a bubble. Some people use it as an unconscious stress reliever, akin to squeezing a stress ball, but more satisfying with the 'pop' announcing your success! Just make sure you don't use up the office supply, and perhaps save it for special times of anticipatory stress. Or take your frustration out wholeheartedly on a sheet. You can also jump on the bubbles and get in some aerobics!

Schedule Another 5 Minutes

If you've tried one of these 5 minute strategies, and still feel stressed, try another one, or do one a second time, as long as time allows. A great pre-emptive strategy is to plan to do a 5 minute tension-zapper every hour or two to insure you feel your best.

What do you have to lose? (Maybe some stress?) And so much more to gain...

5 Minutes Outside

Choose one or more of these awesome, fun, outside the house and office activities to shed the indoor stresses.

Deep Breathing

Typically my first go-to calming activity is deep breathing. If you already do this when you get angry or nervous, or when you meditate or do yoga, you know how calming it can be. And what could be easier? You can do it anywhere.

Sitting or lying down are both great options to do this exercise, Sit or lie down in a comfortable place, feet on the floor (or stretched out straight), arms relaxed at your sides or in your lap. If you can close your eyes it will help shut out the distractions.

Take a deep breath in slowly through your nose as you count to five. Hold for a few counts, and then slowly exhale through your mouth for a count of five. As you inhale, you can say to yourself (in your head) any word or phrase which will calm you. Examples: Calm, Relax, In with Calm, Peace, I'm relaxing now, and so on.

As you exhale, say to yourself one of these or a similar phrase: Letting Go, Stress is leaving, Relaxed, Out with pain/stress/anxiety.

Repeat the inhale/exhale process at least 10 times and you should start to feel more relaxed. A plus is that deep breathing like this also lowers your blood pressure and delivers more oxygen to your body which helps you be healthier in a variety of ways. Take a blood pressure reading before and after to see if it's true for you!

Probably best NOT to do this while driving, especially with your eyes closed!

Watch the Sunset

If you are near a great westerly-facing vantage point, settle in to watch the sun slowly melt into the horizon. One favorite place near me is a local winery which advertises as a great sunset spot. A group of us would go there with a picnic and drink some wine, eat and anticipate the moment separating day from night. It would get quiet and tranquil, until it passed, and then there would be applause for the beauty Mother Nature provides for us daily, if we look. Who can feel stressed while witnessing this amazing show? If you haven't watched the sunset in, well, longer than you can remember, make a point to do this soon, even if you aren't stressed. You'll still feel more peaceful or inspired afterward.

Watch the Sunrise

If you are suffering from stress so that it keeps you awake, or awakens you early, why not take your favorite morning beverage outside and face eastward in preparation for the official beginning of a new day. Be present and watch the transformation of dark to creeping light until finally sunlight erases all the darkness. Imagine the light erasing all your worries and stress. This is a brand new day, one that you can welcome and set an intention to enjoy. Let the sun give you warmth and fresh eyes.

Look for Something

If you find yourself outside without a purpose, perhaps giving yourself one can help you switch gears and let go of what ails you. Try to find something unusual or interesting. It could be an interesting bug or animal, or an item left by someone else. I once found a beetle rolling a nut or pod larger than itself across the gravel road. I had to watch, it was fascinating. Keep looking until you find something you think qualifies as interesting. If you find trash, perhaps pick it up and dispose of it. You'll feel better for being kind to nature.

Smell the Roses (Flowers)

Undoubtedly you've heard people say you need to stop and smell the roses, meaning slow down and be present to what's happening around you. You can take this idea literally if you have fragrant flowers nearby, take a deep breath and enjoy the scent. Close your eyes and imagine you are in a place where flowers are abundant, perhaps a tropical island or rainforest. Put yourself there in your mind while continuing to breathe in the floral magic. Our sense of smell is one of the most readily tied to feelings and situations in our past. Flowers can take you to a beautiful place and memory, so why not enjoy the mini-trip.

Or, you could also entertain this challenge as taking a few minutes to look around you and be present, wherever you are right now. Really look at everything, slowly recognizing each object before moving on to the next. Some items may prompt thoughts of past experiences, or current stresses. Take a moment and let go of the feeling connected to the items that give you stress, before moving on. This can quiet your mind, and clear your thoughts.

Face the Sun

We all know that getting a daily dose of vitamin D is good for us. Of course it is great for keeping our bones strong, but also for lowering blood pressure, fighting off cancers and stalling diabetes, just for a start. And of course the best way to get Vitamin D is from the sun. Take a few minutes (wear your sunscreen) and be outside in the sun. Close your eyes and tilt your face up to the sun, feel the warmth and light fill you. It might even bring a smile to your face as you think about all the great times you've had outside in the sun. Good for what ails you now, and keeping you healthier tomorrow.

Lie Down and Watch the Clouds

Do you remember as a kid (or last week...) lying in the grass and watching the clouds roll by? The idea was to find fun shapes in the clouds. Maybe you were with a child, a parent or a friend, and you'd point out all the objects you'd see. It was fun and relaxing. You can still do this today, and given the type of clouds in the sky, you can look for shapes, or if it's clouded over, just watching the movement of the clouds as the various layers flow over each other. I recently did this and was surprised to see dozens of birds high up in the sky dancing their way through the clouds. Another time I saw the shape of a dog, complete with tail and shaggy ears in the space between the clouds. More fun and relaxing than counting sheep. And you get to dust off your imagination.

Be a kid again...

Star-Gazing

This is best achieved if you live away from the city lights and can find a calm, comfortable spot to sit/lie down. Unless it's an overcast night, you should still see some stars, planets, moons, and who knows what else? Perhaps you'll be fortunate enough to see a shooting star, and make a wish. I have been to a few fantastic places to star-gaze, and will relish the memories as some of the most awe-inspiring.

One night while traveling in the mountains of Pakistan, we slept under the stars at around 10,000 ft. The vista of the heavens was immense, the stars seemed close enough to grasp, and the group of us counted shooting stars until we fell asleep. As I recall we counted nearly 30.

Another was a visit to the McDonald observatory in far west Texas- middle of nowhere- ironically making it one of the best places to see stars. Even better is having a guide who, with his laser pointer, describes the constellations and interesting facts about the sky. This information is useful later when impressing others as to your astronomy prowess.

The idea behind star-gazing is to see the universe as vast and beautiful and mysterious, rendering your stresses of the day rather insignificant. And, probably pretty easy to let go.

Stargazing, anyone?

Walk Barefoot

When I was a kid, it was pretty normal to run around outside barefoot. Nowadays, not so much for most people except at the beach. We worry about what might be in the yard or the dirt. Glass, germs, dog gifts, bugs, garbage, you name it, it could be there. But one of the great things about walking barefoot is connecting to the earth. If this sounds silly to you, try it one day.

Pick a day when the sun has warmed the ground and feel the grass or the dirt -soft or hard- under your feet. Pick another day when there is dew on the grass, and it is cool and wet to your foot. Just pay attention to how your foot experiences the sensations. So very different than with shoes on, you may have forgotten how great it can feel, how freeing.

While you pay attention to your connection to mother earth, she just may encourage you to feel like a kid again.

Summersault, anyone?

Stand in the Rain

With or without an umbrella, standing or walking in the rain can be cleansing, to your body and mind. As long as it's not a lightning storm, the sound of rain falling is very soothing, even mesmerizing. You can buy soundtracks of rain or thunderstorms and listen to them when you want to relax. Combine the rain with breathing deeply and feel the tension fall away.

If you don't want to get wet, and are without umbrella, it's also wonderful to stand or sit on a porch or covered patio and listen to the rain. This was where you would find my son and me when it would rain (an anomaly in the Hill Country some seasons), and enjoy it together. Rocking chairs are perfect for quiet moments like this.

You may hear the call from a nearby puddle...

Schedule Another 5 Minutes

If you've tried one of these 5 minute strategies, and still feel stressed, try another one, or do one a second time, as long as time allows. A great pre-emptive strategy is to plan to do a 5 minute tension-zapper every hour or two to insure you feel your best.

What do you have to lose? (A few years' worth of stress, anxiety, worry, pain...)

There's so much more to gain...

3. When You Have 30 Minutes

When you have more time to devote to kicking out the stress, you have some different and exciting options. 30 minutes can be a mini-vacation when you use them to relax and rejuvenate yourself. Enjoy these great ways to get that done. It may sound like a lot of time for your busy schedule, but you're so worth it.

30 Minutes At Home

These great tips can get you feeling like your best self, lightning-quick. You have all the necessary paraphernalia handy. And nobody is watching, so just go all out. The dog won't tell anybody. The cat may even join in.

Get Moving

Get moving can be interpreted any way you like. The idea is to get up, move about, and get the blood pumping to energize you. You could dance around your living room, do some jumping jacks, toe touches, knee bends, or pull out the vacuum cleaner or broom and clean up as you move. Sometimes, just a change of perspective is all that's needed to wake you up and work out some kinks.

I tend to dance around the living room, sometimes with a cat. Great exercise, and a creative endeavor as well. You never know what fantastic new idea may pop into your mind.

Be open.

Phone a Friend

This 21st century has changed so many things about how we interact with people. Many people prefer to communicate by email or text. But have you noticed how difficult those options are to have a meaningful conversation? A real conversation with give and take, emotional cues, and laughter.

Nothing beats in person communication, but when you can't see someone who you know will help you snap out of a stress-filled state, give them a call. Or Skype. You may also be the perfect diversion for them. Chances are you will find yourself feeling better, and wonder, *Why don't I do this more often?*

Great question. You may want to highlight this one for future reminders...

Take a Cat Nap

I'm not entirely sure why they call a quick nap a 'cat nap', since I've been around cats all my life, and it seems to me that they can sleep indefinitely, and only wake up to the sound of food being opened, or to physical coaxing.

Regardless, when you have 30 minutes, and you feel exhausted, it's the perfect time for a short, but extremely beneficial nap. To get the most benefit, find a comfortable spot, could be your bed, or a favorite couch or lounge chair.

Remove as many distractions as possible (unless the TV helps you fall asleep, then by all means tune it to the most boring channel for you), including streaming light on your face. I recently acquired a fantastic eye mask on a flight on Emirates Airlines and now find that I sleep much more soundly. Try this if you have trouble sleeping during the day. If you need to watch your time, set a timer or alarm for 30 minutes, and then let go.

If it helps, you can try to empty your mind, or tell yourself to relax, or sleep to encourage rest. Chances are, you'll fall asleep easily, and awaken more refreshed, and better able to handle the days' challenges.

Unless the cat woke you up early...

People-Watch

This is one of my favorite pastimes. Before airports stopped letting non-ticketed passengers go to the gates, I loved going to the airport to pick someone up, and always got there early enough to get a great seat and watch the abundance and variety of humanity walk by. If you haven't witnessed loved ones returning (especially military) to joyful, sometimes tearful welcomes, you are missing out. The movie, *Love Actually*, has a fantastic montage of photos of just this, the reuniting of loved ones. Heartwarming, to be sure, and also evidence of how much we all have in common.

So, find a spot to watch some people, look out a window on a busy street, sit at an outdoor café, or find a spot in the mall. Then, just watch. Try not to judge what you see, but just observe. If someone makes you smile, or chuckle, all the better. The idea is to see that there is so much life going on around you, and no matter what your stressors may be right now, in reality they are just like what millions of others experience. This is not to discount what you feel, but only to show you that there are so many other experiences you have had, and will have that are wonderful. This too shall pass. And maybe by watching, you made someone else smile, too. You could be someone else's example of happiness tomorrow.

Gratitude List

We all have blessings in our lives. Oftentimes, especially in times of stress or trauma, we may not think we have any. This is the best time to take stock of all the great people and abundance we enjoy.

If you haven't done this before, it's exceedingly simple. Pull out a clean sheet of paper, and your favorite writing utensil (this is much more effective if you write by hand, but if you MUST do it electronically, print it out when you've finished your list).

Just ask yourself this question, *What am I grateful for?* Write it at the top of your page, and then just let the answers pour out of you. Don't worry about the order, the spelling, or whether you believe it or not, just write what comes to mind uncensored.

Give yourself about 15 minutes to think and write. Set a timer. Once the time is up, or when you feel you've exhausted your list, look it over. Just read it, and think about what each person or gift on your list has meant to you. Perhaps revisit how you came to receive this gift. Then, for each item say out loud, or to yourself, thank you for this wonderful blessing of-*fill in the blank*-in my life. Repeat this for every item on your list.

Now, how do you feel? Pretty darn lucky, right? Nothing else is as important as these blessings.

Remember this, every day.

Soak Your Feet

When your feet ache, it can make you feel tense and achy all over. When I was working retail for the holidays, I would come home and beg anyone to give me a foot rub. Usually there were no takers, so I started soaking my feet in some hot water with Epsom salts. Then, for Christmas, my family gave me a foot bath complete with jets and rolling parts to rub my feet against. It felt heavenly.

You don't have to have the expensive foot bath to reap the same benefits. You will need a big enough pot or bucket to fit your feet inside, and some basic supplies. Warm enough water to the warmest you can handle, add a cup of Epsom salts, and if you like, add a few drops of an essential oil such as lavender, chamomile, or peppermint. Soak your feet until the water cools. This is a great time for a relaxing glass of wine or cup of tea. Dry them, and as you dry, massage the bottoms of your feet, the ball, the arch and the heel. Follow up with some creamy lotion and continue massaging.

Maybe you have someone who would love to pamper you, accept their gift! You will feel like a new person. Cheers!

Play With a Pet/Child

You already know that some of the best videos out there to make you smile involve the antics of small children or pets. There's a reason for this; they don't have censors, they just enjoy the moment.

Sometimes we forget how to do this, so why not spend a half hour learning (remembering) from a master? Hopefully you have one of these masters available to you in your home.

If so, make a point to live in the moment with your little person, favorite feline or canine. You don't need to have an elaborate plan. In fact, if you plan to play with a child, just ask them what they would like to do. They are never at a loss for ideas, so you might find yourself building a pillow fort, or a Lego skyscraper, or dressing up as a princess or superhero. Try not to control the process and just enjoy the moment with them. Remember this simple kind of fun? Yeah, and making new great memories with your little one.

It's the same with your pet, although you may have to get the ball rolling, so to speak. It's as easy as turning on a laser pointer, pulling a string or tossing a ball to get them joining in the fun. Maybe wrestling with your furry Fido, or brushing your pet is more your style. You know what they like, and they may remind you more often than you indulge. My big cat waits for me to sit on my bed at night, jumps up on the bed and stares at me until I pull out the laser pointer and get him running around in circles. If I ignore him, he will start asking me. These small tokens of time can be de-stressing for you, and a joy for both of you.

Clean Something

This is not usually one of my top 20 (or 100) solutions for stress, but I have heard enough other people say it calms them down, and helps them feel in control. If that is you, clean away.

If you don't know if this will help you, my suggestion would be to pick an area of your home that you feel needs help, organizing or weeding out. This could be as simple as a junk drawer or your DVDs/CDs/Books. Or you could take on something that is nagging at you, but you've been putting off, like the refrigerator or the garage.

Whatever you decide to clean, give it your full attention, and give it your best possible effort. Once you commit, you may find ways to complete it easily, and have, dare I say, FUN doing it?

When you are finished, you will no doubt feel quite accomplished and amazingly calmer, as when your living space is in order, so are you. This could even start a trend. Or perhaps a family project...

Stretch/Yoga

Sometimes relaxing only requires stretching your muscles to release the pent up energy stored in them. When your muscles get so tense that they start sending you de-stress signals, one first line of defense is to stretch them out. Work out some of the lactic acid build-up and they will move more freely. If you have just a couple places you feel the stress, work specifically on those.

Yoga poses are amazing for stretching gently, and one overall fantastic stretching pose is a dead man pose. Lie on the floor on your back, legs and arms straight. Just relax each part of your body into the floor, muscle by muscle. Start at your feet and deliberately relax your feet, then your calves, thighs, and so on up to your head. As you pay attention to each part, you will feel the release, until you just melt into the floor.

If you can't lie on the floor, another way to stretch your body is to stand with your feet shoulder width apart, hold on to a table or couch for balance and bend over at the waist until you feel the stretch in your back and legs. Then let your head and arms dangle. Hold this and breathe deeply. As you relax and your muscles unkink, you will sink lower to the ground. Hold as long as comfortable. Do this periodically throughout the day as you start to feel tense.

There are so many great videos for Yoga and Stretching. You can try some out on Netflix or Amazon Prime before buying ones that you enjoy. I have one video that has three ten minute yoga workouts, one for morning, one for evening and one specifically for stress reduction. They usually recommend using a yoga mat (so you don't slip in some of the poses), and sometimes a strap, but in a pinch you can use the carpet with bare feet and a towel. Quick, easy and very effective.

Om...

Light a Scented Candle

Fragrances can induce feelings, good or bad, based on experiences you have related to a particular smell. For instance, when you smell freshly mown grass, what do you think of or feel? Or how about the scent of cookies baking? Yep, gotcha.

The candle can be a simple reminder of a time that makes you feel good, or a scent that has inherent soothing benefits. You just have to have on hand a few of the scents that you know will help you chill out. If you haven't been to a candle shop in a long time, you are in for a treat. You can find scented candles ranging from chocolate chip cookie, to ocean breeze to pina colada.

Light up one or many to encourage great feelings.

Take a Bath

This is one of my favorite ways to relax and shut out the rest of the world. All you need is your favorite bath oil or bubbles, add some Epsom salts if you have sore muscles, and the warmest water you can stand.

Make sure the rest of your household knows you are unavailable for the duration. Place a DO NOT DISTURB sign on the bathroom door if that will help. Then add some of your favorite items for ambiance. Use candles, soft music, a glass of wine, your latest novel, or anything else you like.

This is not meant to be work, so just relax, let the water soak away your cares....

What cares?

Massage Your Feet

This one is similar to the Soak Your Feet, but you don't need to have the water and other required implements handy. Of course, the perfect solution would be to have someone else massage your feet for you. If you are such a blessed person, take advantage of it. When my kids were still at home, I used to rub my daughter's back and shoulders, sometimes in exchange for a foot rub. Heavenly. I live alone now, and haven't yet figured out how to get the cat to do this (especially without using claws) for me.

If you are the one to do it, no problem, you will know what feels the best. Just rub along the bottom and top slowly and deeply, long strokes and circles. Pay attention to the places which feel tight or sore, and be tender. Your feet are connected to all parts of your body, so taking care of them also helps heal the rest of you.

You'll never ignore your feet again!

Schedule Another 30 Minutes

If you've tried one of these 30 minute strategies, and still feel stressed, try another one, or do one a second time, as long as time allows. A great pre-emptive strategy is to put a 30 minute block of Less-Stress time on your calendar every day to keep stress at bay. At the very least, incorporate a 5 minute tension-zapper every hour or two to insure you feel your best.

What do you have to lose? (Maybe a bit of stress?) There's so much more to gain...

30 Minutes At Work

If you can wrangle a half hour during lunch or a break, these simple and effective distractions can be lifesavers at work. Keep your sanity (or find it again!) by breaking out of the stress cycle. Do it for you. And your co-workers...

Get Moving

Get moving can be interpreted anyway you would like. The idea is to get up, move about, and get the blood pumping to energize you. You could dance around your office, assuming you have privacy, you don't want to start a flash mob (or maybe you do...). Or you could do some jumping jacks, toe touches, knee bends, or wall push-ups. Since you have 30 minutes, you could walk around, or even better combine the walking with some calisthenics. Sometimes, just a change of perspective is all that's needed to wake you up and work out some kinks.

Be sure you are not sitting at your desk, and find a way to get moving. It's great exercise, and a creative endeavor as well. You never know what great idea may pop into your mind.

Be open to action.

Phone a Friend

This 21st century has changed so many things about how we interact with people. Many people prefer to communicate by email, or text. But have you noticed how difficult those options are to have a meaningful conversation? With give and take, emotional cues, and laughter.

Nothing beats in-person communication, but when you can't see someone who you know will help you snap out of a stress-filled state, give them a call. Or Skype with them. You may also be the perfect diversion for them. Chances are you will find yourself feeling better, and wonder, *Why don't I do this more often?*

A-ha! You may want to highlight this one for future reminders…

People Watch

This is one of my favorite pastimes. Before airports stopped letting non-ticketed passengers go to the gates, I loved going to the airport to pick someone up, and always got there early enough to get a great seat and watch the abundance and variety of humanity walk by. If you haven't witnessed loved ones returning (especially military) to joyful, sometimes tearful welcomes, you are missing out. The movie, *Love Actually*, has a fantastic montage of photos of just this, the reuniting of loved ones. Heartwarming, to be sure, and also evidence of how much we all have in common.

So, find a spot to watch some people, look out a window on a busy street, sit at an outdoor café, or find a spot in the lobby. Then, just watch. Try not to judge what you see, but just observe. If someone makes you smile, or chuckle, all the better. The idea is to see that there is so much life going on around you, no matter what your stressors may be right now, in reality they are just like what millions of others experience. This is not to discount what you feel, but only to remind you that there are so many other great experiences you have had, and will have. This too shall pass.

And maybe by watching, you made someone else smile, too. You could be someone else's' example of happiness tomorrow.

Gratitude List

We all have blessings in our lives. Oftentimes, especially in times of high stress or trauma, we may not think we have any good, only problems. This is the best time to take stock of all the great people and abundance we have.

If you haven't done this before, it's exceedingly simple. Pull out a clean sheet of paper, and your favorite writing implement (this is much more effective if you write with your hand, but if you MUST do it electronically, print it out when you've finished your list).

Just ask yourself this question, *What am I grateful for?* Write it at the top of your page, and then just let the answers pour out of you. Don't worry about the order, the spelling, or whether you believe it or not, just write uncensored what comes to mind.

Give yourself about 15 minutes to think and write. Set a timer. Once the time is up, or when you feel you've exhausted your list, look it over. Just read it, and think about what each person or gift on your list has meant to you. Perhaps revisit how you came to receive this gift. Then, for each item say out loud, or to yourself, thank you for this wonderful blessing of-*fill in the blank*-in my life. Repeat this for every item on your list.

Now, how do you feel? Pretty darn lucky, right? Nothing else is as important as these blessings.

Remember this, *every day*.

Go for a Drive

As I write this section, it is a gorgeous September day in the Texas Hill Country. 80 degrees, the sun is shining, no humidity and a fabulous breeze. The perfect type of weather to make me itch to get in the car, open the sunroof or roll down the windows, crank up some great tunes and drive the winding country roads.

Nothing can take me away from the everyday ho-hum and get me smiling quite like a drive. Is this true for you? You don't need to have a destination in mind, but you could end up at your favorite coffee shop or café, or your favorite lookout point to sit and ponder life.

You don't even need the perfect weather, but you may want to pick a time or route that won't be gridlocked with traffic, which would only add to your stress. Even then, you can still sing along at the top of your lungs and smile at the neighboring drivers. It's the *get-away-from-it-all* factor that can help you reboot. And of course your choice of *make-you-happy* tunes.

Watch out for the speed traps...

Clean Something

This is not usually one of my top 20 (or 100...) solutions for stress, but I have heard enough other people say that cleaning calms them down, and helps them feel in control. If that is you, clean away.

If you don't know if this will help you, my suggestion would be to pick an area of your office space that you feel needs help, organizing or weeding out. This could be as simple as cleaning off the top of your desk, or deleting your voicemails . Or you could take on something that is nagging at you, but you've been putting off, like the file cabinet or the rolodex (or the 21st century equivalent).

Whatever you decide to clean, give it your full attention, and give it your best possible effort. Once you commit, you may find ways to complete it easily, and dare I say, have FUN doing it?

When you are finished, you will no doubt feel quite accomplished and amazingly calmer, as when your working space is in order, so are you. This could even start a trend.

Or perhaps a co-worker rescue program...

Stretch/Yoga

Sometimes relaxing only requires stretching your muscles to release the pent up energy stored in them. When your muscles get so tense that they start sending you de-stress signals, one first line of defense is to stretch them out. Work out some of the lactic acid build-up and they will move more freely. If you have just a couple places you feel the stress, work specifically on those.

Yoga poses are amazing for stretching gently, and one overall fantastic stretching pose is a dead man pose. If you have room, lie on the floor on your back, legs and arms straight. Just relax each part of your body into the floor, muscle by muscle. Start at your feet and deliberately relax your feet, then your calves, thighs, and so on up to your head. As you pay attention to each part, you will feel the release, until you just melt into the floor.

If you can't lie on the floor, another way to stretch your body is to stand with your feet shoulder width apart, and bend over at the waist until you feel the stretch in your back and legs. Let your head and arms dangle. Hold this and breathe deeply. As you relax and your muscles unkink, you will sink lower to the ground. Hold as long as comfortable. Do this periodically throughout the day as you start to feel tense.

There are so many great videos for Yoga and Stretching. You can try some out on Netflix or Amazon Prime before buying ones that you enjoy. I have one that has three ten minute yoga workouts, one for morning, one for evening and one specifically for stress reduction. They recommend a yoga mat, and sometimes a strap, but you can use the carpet and a towel in a pinch. Quick, easy and very effective.

Om...

Light a Scented Candle

Fragrances can induce feelings, good or bad, based on experiences you have related to a particular smell. For instance, when you smell freshly mown grass, what do you think of or feel? How about the scent of cookies baking? Yep, *gotcha.*

The candle can be a simple reminder of a time that makes you feel good, or a scent that has inherent soothing benefits. You just have to have on hand a few of the scents that you know will help you chill out.

If you haven't been to a candle shop in a long time, you are in for a treat. You can find scented candles ranging from chocolate chip cookie, to ocean breeze to piña colada. Make sure you pick up a couple that are known to be calming, like lavender, ocean scents, chamomile and for most people pie scented ones.

Enjoy!

Help Someone

Take a moment to think about whether there is someone at work who you know is struggling with something with which you could help. They may or may not have asked for help, but you feel that you may be able to make their life easier.

Approach them and offer your assistance or guidance in a way that is non-threatening. You've been there yourself, and wanted to make the task easier for them through your prior learning. You are offering yourself as a temporary mentor, and when you help someone else succeed, you feel pretty good as well.

For a little while, you didn't think about your own stresses. With a new successful assist, you feel ready to take on your own challenges with a brighter perspective.

You paid it forward, and you never know when it may come back to you.

Take a Break

This is a deliberate break from whatever you're doing (unless you are 'in the zone') just to clear your head, perhaps stand up (or sit down) and stretch out your muscles. Set a timer, and forget everything until it rings. No, no cheating. *Let it go.*

~Stress-Less in 5 Minutes~

Write Down Your Stress

This is a stress version of writing a letter to someone and then tearing it up. The idea is to sit and write out whatever is bothering you, causing you stress. Just let it free-flow out of you and on to the paper. No censoring, ideally spend 10 or 15 minutes exhausting the topic.

You may ask yourself any of these questions to get you started:

- What is making me so stressed?
- Who is adding to my stress?
- What am I doing that is making me feel bad?
- What else is going on in my life that is stressful?
- How could these stressors be related?
- How could I lessen some of it?
- Who could help me?
- What one thing could I do today to stop it?

These should give you enough to get the ball rolling. When you feel like you've put it all down on paper, check to see how you feel. Are you exhausted, exhilarated, angry, or relieved? Do you see anything surprising? If you didn't, answer the last question, what one thing could you do today?

Now, if you like, rip up the paper into as many pieces as you can and toss them. Put it through the shredder. Burn it. Whatever helps you "get rid" of the evidence and quite likely a good deal of the stress.

Take a deep breath, and move on to that one thing you can do now…

Visualize a Peaceful Place

Think of visualizing like daydreaming. We all do it, perhaps even today during that meeting about nothing, which only took time away from what you needed to get done. You zoned out and started thinking about the weekend, going to see your friend and playing out in your mind's eye what will happen. That's visualization. You're already a master at it.

Now, however, you want to use this skill to help calm and release the stress you are feeling. You have 30 minutes to work with, so first take out some paper and pen and write at the top: Places I Love or Places that are Peaceful. Then just brainstorm places known/or unknown that fit the bill for you. It might be the beach where you went on your honeymoon, or what you imagine what it would be like to sit in a treehouse up in the canopy of a rainforest. Places you would love to go, or have pictures you would like to insert yourself into.

Do this brainstorming for a few minutes, or until you exhaust your list. Next, pick one to use now as your peaceful place. If you do have a picture available of this place, take it out and start there.

Get comfortable where you are, close your eyes and paint the picture you have in your mind. If you don't have a picture handy, make one up that fits your chosen place. Use as much detail as you can; *What colors do you see? Are there shades of color in the trees, water, flowers, buildings, or people? What do you smell? Do you smell food, flowers, sea spray? What sounds do you hear? Traffic noises, people chatter, music, birds, the rolling ocean waves? What do you feel? Is there a breeze caressing your skin, or the sun warming your face, or water lapping against your body? Are there people with you or around you? What are they doing? What are you doing?*

Fill in as much of the picture as you can, using all your senses. Put yourself into this place and move around it. Spend as much time as you need to relax and enjoy yourself.

This is your special peaceful place, make it your sanctuary that you can return to any time and feel the calm release of your current stress. You may want to set a timer so you come back in time for your next meeting...

May the Peace be with You.

Meditate

Meditation is a practice of concentrated focus upon a sound, object, visualization, your breath, or movement in order to increase awareness of the present moment, reduce stress, promote relaxation, and enhance personal and spiritual growth. Sounds like just what the doctor ordered. If you've never tried it, give it a few chances to notice the benefits. It gets easier and more enjoyable with practice.

The process is easy and painless, so sit back and enjoy! First, turn off or silence any possible distractions. Next, decide if you want to concentrate on your breathing, or repeating a word (such as Calm, Relax, or Om) either in your head or out loud. The idea is to focus on one of these two things instead of any other thoughts or distractions.

Find a comfortable chair and sit with both feet planted firmly on the floor. Or sit on the floor with your legs comfortably crossed, knees out to the sides. Sit in a position that you feel you could hold for the duration of the meditation- in this case 20 to 30 minutes.

Close your eyes and relax as much as you can.

Breathe deeply, paying attention to your breath, in for four counts, and then out for four counts. If you plan to concentrate on your breath, continue to count it in and out. If you decide to focus on a word (mantra), repeat the word to yourself on every exhale.

As you go along, thoughts will come into your mind, try to let them go without much attention and continue with your attention to your breath or mantra. This will happen repeatedly, but just brush the intruding thoughts aside for now. Concentrate on breathing and you will find yourself relaxing more as time goes by.

When your timer rings, and your time for meditation is over, remain still until you feel ready to open your eyes.

Take a minute to jot down thoughts, feelings, or images you experienced during the session. This is a great habit to start after meditation, because you may have solutions to problems come out of it, or creative insights to pursue later. You will feel more relaxed, and perhaps more clear-headed and energized. Whatever you now need to address may suddenly seem less an obstacle and more an interesting endeavor.

That's it! Easy, but very effective.

Read an Inspiring or Humorous Book

One great rule of thumb I have, and you may want to adopt, is to never be caught without something to read. Whether it's a paperback or graphic novel that fits into your purse or pocket, or digital books you can read on a kindle, cell phone or laptop. When you need a break from work, break out a book that will make you smile or provide the inspiration to keep going.

Reading can be a catalyst for great ideas. Laughter can be what turns your mood from sour to sweet, spilling over into the rest of your day. Thirty minutes of reading can transport you to another time, place, world or mindset. Pretend you are the hero/heroine for a while, bringing with you the courage, ingenuity and humanity found in the character.

Choose books that will make that trip a positive, fun and inspiring one.

Superhero cape not included.

Schedule Another 30 Minutes

If you've tried one of these 30 minute strategies, and still feel stressed, try another one, or do one a second time, as long as time allows. A great pre-emptive strategy is to put a 30 minute block of Less-Stress time on your calendar every day to keep stress at bay. At the very least, incorporate a 5 minute tension-zapper every hour or two to insure you feel your best.

~Stress-Less in 5 Minutes~

What do you have to lose? (Stress, perhaps?) There's so much more to gain...

30 Minutes Outside

Ahh, the great outdoors. The perfect place to let go of all that brings you down. Soak in all the healing available from Mother Nature as often as you can. It's waiting for you...

Go Hiking

Walking is just about the best exercise available. Not that long ago, it wasn't even considered exercise, it was just what you did to get around. Of course that was before we could drive everywhere, even buy food, do the banking and wash the car, without ever having to step out of the vehicle. Now, unless you live in Downtown, Large City, Anywhere, chances are you don't have to walk that much during the day. So, we strap on pedometers and fancy fitness bracelets and attempt to recreate the type of walking we used to do naturally.

Hiking is walking, but generally on a scenic route, perhaps with variable terrain and best done with the appropriate boots/shoes and if you like, a cool walking stick. When you want to be outside, why not take advantage of the many vistas available when you walk a park trail? You will soak up some Vitamin D, see some interesting flora and fauna and perhaps even meet your daily pedometer goal. Oh, and you'll also feel better. With each step, let go of the stress and soak in the fresh air. You may lose track of time, but not the benefits of the hike!

Adventures await you...

Plant Something

What could be more rewarding than adding beauty to your environment? Depending on what time of year it is, and your supplies on hand, what to plant will vary. Planting a tree can be exciting, especially if you plan to live in the same place for many more years, or in the neighborhood. The idea of 'putting down roots' in the literal sense can bring you years of joy as you watch it grow.

Flowers are also fun, mixing your favorite colors and varieties. If it's winter, you can always plant a pot of flowers to place in a window and enjoy when all else outside is wintry gray. If you don't have time to make the trip to a nursery, most people have plants that could use some pruning, deadheading or separating to encourage more growth.

Whatever you decide, get your fingers in the dirt, connect to the earth and help something grow. You'll feel accomplished and have a reminder of your efforts every time you see what you've done! If you're feeling especially connected to your plant (like my daughter who planted a lime tree and named it Steve), pick a name for it, and on later stress-reducing activities, talk to it, talk out your stress.

Just be careful not to yell or curse at it, plants have feelings too.

Wash the Car

Depending on the weather, this can be a great way to get a tan while giving your vehicle a bit of TLC. Generally, I persuade the kids to do this for me, which can take an hour or more and numerous buckets of water. This time, it's for you to let off some steam. Physical activity is a wonderful way to do that, and why not get a sparkling car out of the time and effort?

Assemble all the tools you'll need ahead of time, to prevent frustration at having to make multiple trips retrieving what you need- bucket, sponge, rags, towels, soap, tire or chrome cleaner, and any other items you will use.

Put your whole effort into the experience, concentrating on enjoying making your car look much better than any drive-through wash will do.

When you're finished, take it out for a spin, or at least a selfie.

Sunbathe

This one is easy, but 30 minutes may seem like a long time if you are sensitive to the sun, so make sure you have the appropriate sunscreen applied before you go out. You only need 10 minutes of sunlight to get your daily requirement of Vitamin D, but this is to put a bit of color in your cheeks, maybe a bit of sun streaking for your hair, and the chance to relax, do nothing but soak up some rays. You don't even have to wear a swim suit! Just whatever you're wearing is fine. It's a great time to do some deep breathing if you are especially tense, or to listen to some relaxing music. Or just close your eyes and pay attention to the sounds of whatever is happening in nature around you.

All of these activities will help you relax, and get your bearings back.

Play Something

Stress tends to evaporate when we play. And it's pretty fun. You're outside already, might as well take advantage of the wide open space.

Maybe you're near a park and can play on the swings or slide. Maybe there's a basketball hoop and you can play with others. Or a backboard to hit tennis balls against.

If you're alone without any equipment, you can make up a game, like finding something that starts with each letter of the alphabet. Or you might find yourself twirling, jumping, hopping, skipping or turning cartwheels just like you used to as a kid.

It's all about having some fun, and forgetting about what concerns you, for a short while anyway.

Let out your inner child and PLAY!

Read a Book for Fun

I try not to leave home without something to read. It's easier since the invention of electronic readers, tablets and even smart phones, but I also enjoy the feel of the pages in an *old-fashioned* book.

The key for this activity is to read something that will somehow calm you down. Whether you pick a book that inspires, makes you laugh or engrosses you in solving a mystery, the beauty of reading is that it transports you away from your present place and all that comes with it, to another, different place where you can laugh, slay dragons or fall in love.

Guaranteed to rewrite your current stress.

Don't leave home without one.

Sit by Water

Outdoors is a great place to let go of the small and human trouble we have. Being near water is even better. Ever notice how dentist offices and therapist offices frequently have fish tanks? They know that the sound of the bubbles and watching the fish calms down waiting patients.

If you have a lake, ocean or even a flowing stream nearby, head out to be soothed by the sound of water rushing, rolling in or trickling by. You may find a spot to sit and close your eyes concentrating only on the sound of water.

As a kid, I would go to sit by a river across the street from my home whenever I wanted to sort out a problem, or to temper anger and frustration. It didn't take long to feel mesmerized by its movement, almost sweeping away my cares. I also found that if I stayed long enough, and posed a question about my current problem, answers would come.

Calm restored, and solutions provided. Ready to move forward!

Connect to the Earth

Since the invention of shoes, most of us don't spend much (if any) time outside barefoot. Most of the time this makes sense, but we've lost our connection to the earth, being grounded. Literally. When was the last time you walked outside (not on concrete, or a deck) and felt the cool grass on your feet, got dirt or sand between your toes?

Well, today, right now is your chance to do it again. Do you remember in the movie *Pretty Woman,* when Richard Gere goes outside and sits down in his expensive suit, takes off his shoes and socks and walks around? People think he's a little nuts, but for him, it's a chance to *feel* connected to his childhood, happy days, to our planet. It may sound nuts, but you'll find when you are connected to Mother Nature through direct contact, you are also connected to her infinite wisdom and peace.

So, go outside, sit, stand or lie down on the ground and get connected with your feet, hands, or head, and just be still for a while drinking in the stillness of the earth.

Trust me, you'll love it. And if you have kids, they likely already do it, so you can do it together.

Go for a Drive

Unless driving is inherently stressful for you, a drive with no destination or pressure can be quite relaxing. This option is dependent on the weather, so pick a day that is fair and dry outside. The season isn't important for they each have beauty to enjoy while on the road. The key is to take the back roads. Stay off the expressways, and take the scenic route, the roads less travelled. If it's nice enough, open the windows or the sun roof, crank up the tunes and sing your heart out. Nobody can hear you. You can even dance with your head.

Soak up the experience, and have a great trip!

Write in a Journal

One of my favorite places to write is outside. The only distractions are nature and the resident critters. While they certainly can be a distraction, I find them to be a welcome one, providing inspiration, laughs and even topics for journaling.

Take your favorite journal and writing implement and find a comfortable spot, in your yard, a park, anywhere that you enjoy the ambiance. If you want, write about what issues are causing you stress. 30 minutes may seem like a long time, but once you start it will probably fly by. You can also write about your hopes and dreams for the next few months. Observe the flora and fauna around and write about that. Free write what pops into your head, although watch out for hand cramps!

If you run out of things to say before your time runs out, go back and read what you've written. You may find nuggets of insight or solutions to problems that have stumped you. You may feel blessed and happy. These are all benefits of writing down what seems to be on your mind. Use this whenever you want to have a conversation with yourself.

Being outside adds the wisdom of nature to the process. Mother Nature knows things.

Have a Picnic

Even a picnic for one can be a rewarding, enjoyable experience. It involves a bit of planning, but it doesn't have to be fancy. The basic requirements would include something to sit on, a blanket, towel or table cloth, something to eat (preferably finger foods) and something to drink (even as simple as bottled water or a juice box). Take time to savor the experience, tasting your food and enjoying the sights, smells and sounds around you.

You can nourish your stomach and your soul while adding some calm to your day. Now, find a scenic spot, spread out your feast and enjoy.

Be a good scout and leave no trace of your visit behind!

Go to the Beach

If you are lucky enough to live near an ocean, the beach is a fantastic place to let go of some stress. No matter the season, the beach offers the same rolling waves and cacophony of seagulls to lull you into a less frenetic space.

Sit, stand, walk, or even run along the shore or in the surf. Find a comfortable spot and drink in the sounds, smells, sights and feel of all that's around you. Concentrate on what's going on outside and you won't pay attention to what you're feeling inside. Explore the area for interesting shells, rocks or people.

Whatever you find at the beach, let it help you see the big picture of life, and not dwell so much on the smaller troubles.

You can handle those now.

Draw a Picture (or Take One)

This exercise encourages you to let out your inner artist! The one you may have put away once you left elementary school. Not anymore! Today you unleash your creative side.

You only need something to write on, and something to write with. If you plan ahead, you can keep a small art supply bag with you, filled with notebooks, cardstock, colored pencils/pens, a watercolor set, or anything else you like to use.

The plan is to draw a picture of something you find outside where you are. It doesn't have to be gallery-worthy, in fact you don't even have to show anyone else unless you so desire. You just have to see what comes out as you admire nature, and interpret it on paper.

And of course, have fun!

If all you have with you is a phone with a camera, or a regular camera, try to find an interesting shot or two of something interesting. You may post it on social media, or make it your computer wallpaper.

You may find yourself looking for more opportunities to create something lovely. It's hard to feel bad when you look for the beauty around you.

Schedule Another 30 Minutes

If you've tried one of these 30 minute strategies, and still feel stressed, try another one, or do one a second time, as long as time allows. A great pre-emptive strategy is to put a 30 minute block of Less-Stress time on your calendar every day to keep stress at bay. At the very least, incorporate a 5 minute tension-zapper every hour or two to insure you feel your best.

What do you have to lose? (Unwanted Stress, perhaps?) There's so much more to gain...

4. When You Have 1+ Hour

A whole hour to de-stress your life; sounds heavenly, doesn't it? You can work out a lot of kinks and knots in an hour. You can change your mood, your location, even your future in an hour. Let's do that now...

1 Hour At Home

Here are some great tricks for getting rid of stress at home. Build one or more into your day however works best, but be sure to let go of (or silence, cover up, let outside...) all the stuff at home to distract you. This time is all about you.

Watch a Funny Movie/Show

Laughter is one of the secrets to a long and healthy life. If you or someone you live with aren't stand-up comedians, then the next best way to working out your belly by laughing is to watch something that never fails to have you cackling.

If you own or have access to your favorite films or shows, you can always escape whenever you need your funny fix. If not, you could go to YouTube and watch some funny pet or people videos. They're everywhere. Watch until you find it easier to smile than to frown, and not only will you feel better, you'll look better. You may want to assemble a library of these to keep at the ready.

Go ahead, laugh, it's a great exercise for your abs...

Exercise

If you have a lot of bottled-up energy in the form of stress, why not get rid of it and get in shape at the same time? Especially if you don't belong to a gym, or aren't able to go, it doesn't mean that you can't still get a workout.

You may not want to, but if you knew you would feel better afterward, wouldn't you do it anyway? Just this once? Okay, then. There are an infinite number of ways you can burn off some energy (and calories!), so start with any videos you may have. Dust off the Jane Fonda, Richard Simmons or Jazzercise videos and feel the burn.

If you have any fitness equipment, free weights, kettle bells, yoga straps, treadmill, whatever it may be, take it for a spin. Be sure to warm up first and stretch afterward, but work out some of the stress kinks that have you screaming inside.

There are also many online places to pull up fitness videos, anything from Pilates to Tai Chi to Kickboxing. Great options if you've always wanted to try something new, but didn't want to do it in front of a room full of experts!

Plan Your Dream Vacation

This is one of my favorite activities when I can't leave home. Do you have some place you have always wanted to visit, but just can't seem to make it happen? A great start is to make a plan. Go crazy, research your dream destination online or in travel guides. Find pictures of the sights you want to visit and print them or add them to a Pinterest board.

Research the costs: flights, or gasoline expenses, hotel options, costs of museums or other attractions, food, souvenirs, any and everything you imagine you'll need to plan for on this once in a lifetime trip. Use whatever means makes sense to you to organize it: on a spreadsheet, or a notebook, a poster board, but put it all together. It'll be fun, and make you feel that much closer to actually making the trip.

That'll make the next step easier, setting the date to go…

Bon voyage!

Make a Vision Board

A vision board is a fun and creative way to take your mind off your current problems, and dream about how you want your life to look. When you have pictures that represent what you want in your life, it's easier to imagine having them.

If you're not familiar with the vision board idea, there are as many ways to make one as there are people making them. Start with a basic plan, and gather some poster board or a corkboard, some magazines, catalogs, books and scissors, glue, pushpins or tape. The goal of a vision board is to find visual representations of the things you want to have, be or do in your life, assemble them in one place on a board as a daily inspiration.

Think of all the things that are important to you: the work you (want to) do, the places you want to travel, the car you want to drive, the way you wish to look, the people you have around you, anything that you aspire to in your life.

Start cutting out pictures that meet your ideal goal and attach them to the board. You can also print out pictures from the internet if what you are looking for is hard to find. Be creative, and label each item if you like, or add thought bubbles or color around them, have fun with the process.

When you're finished (this may take you more than an hour, so allow for that or plan another session to finish) find a place to display it where you will see it every day. The more you look at it and imagine yourself in the pictures, the faster you will make it happen. You want it, you deserve it, so let go of the stress and see your life-better!

Bake Something

Nothing smells better than something sweet and delicious baking in the oven. Savvy realtors know this and bake cookies for visitors to their open houses. Nothing says home quite like it.

When you bake, you need to concentrate on following the recipe, doing all the steps (my daughter once made brownies without adding the egg, they turned out more like fudge-but still delicious), and naturally you will think less about your stresses. As your creation bakes, let the fabulous aroma calm you and take you to happier, more carefree times.

And then, enjoy your treat. Feel even better if you share some with others!

Make a Donation Pile

Sometimes when our lives seem overwhelming, the simple act of de-cluttering a space where we live can act as a stabilizing force in other areas of our lives. The act of assembling items for donation can itself seem overwhelming, but with only an hour on the clock, the idea is to make a small, manageable difference.

Choose one area, or decide ahead of time a number of items to fill your box or bag, and once you're done, stop. Perhaps it's the end of winter and time to bring out your spring/summer clothes. Before you put away the sweaters, coats and scarves, go through them and decide what you absolutely love, what you want to keep, and what doesn't fit well, you haven't worn all season, or don't really like anymore. Fill your box with the pieces you don't absolutely love. Someone else may love what you give away.

If you have more toys, games, household items than you know where to store them, it's time to weed out the has-been, unused items.

When your hour is up, appreciate what you've accomplished, and the space you have freed up in your home, and your life. One benefit of this is by giving away useful items to others, you invite more great things to come into your life.

Maybe make this a monthly activity...

Finger Paint

Do you remember finger-painting as a child? Or doing it with your own children? If I close my eyes, I can still smell the fragrant colors, feel the slippery wet paint on my fingers. And see a blank sheet of paper with infinite possibilities.

There's something simple and exhilarating about creating with your hands, and nobody expects it to look like a Rembrandt, or even a Picasso. You may use it to paint your frustration, anger, stress! When you let it out, you won't be carrying it around with you. Not to mention, you just might feel like Michelangelo!

Make room on the fridge for your masterpiece!

Read an Inspiring Book

When you're stressed, a book can take you to another place, or invite you to look at things differently. You can read anything that you enjoy that won't make you any more tense. But to really get yourself out of stress-mode, a book that will inspire you to think big, to consider that there is more to this life than surviving the daily grind is what I highly recommend.

If you're not sure what to read, try searching at a library, bookstore or online for Inspirational or Motivational books. They may not be the 'can't put it down until I'm finished' kind of reading, but if you spend an hour with a good uplifting book, you will feel better, and may even have ideas about how to improve your situation.

I imagine you'll even smile once or twice. Try it. And carry the book with you, leave it in the car or your office, for whenever you need a pick-me-up -motivationally.

Enjoy a Hobby $

If you have a favorite hobby, but can't remember the last time you took time to enjoy it, now might be the perfect time to dust it off and indulge. If it's been a very long time, just to refresh your memory, a hobby is an activity in which, while nobody is requiring or paying you to participate, you are completely lost in time when you are doing it.

Examples might be a sport, a club, assembling a collection, an artistic endeavor, learning a language or anything else you can feel lost pursuing. You can do it alone or with a group. The key is to take some time to do something you love.

Once you do, you'll wonder why you ever stopped, and will most likely find it easier to schedule your hobby back into your life.

Which is where it really should be. Take the feeling with you.

Write It Down & Burn It

This can be an extremely cathartic activity. If you are not one who generally likes to write, I encourage you to give it a try at least once. There is also the 'Burn It' part of the process you won't want to miss!

Sometimes, when you have others nearby who will hear you vocally release your frustration, or the walls will allow the words to seep outside your safe space, the next best thing is to write it down, silently. And it may even be your preferred method.

Pull out some old fashioned paper and a pen. You can write using a computer keyboard, but it's much easier and more gratifying to use ink and flourishes to get out your anxiety. (Plus remember that Burn It part...)

Take a minute or more to collect your thoughts, asking yourself, *"What is it that is bothering/frustrating/angering/stressing me?"* Let the question percolate for a bit, until you feel like writing down all that comes to mind.

This is not the time to hold back, just let everything you can think of flow through the pen to the paper. Nobody is going to see it. As you write, you may find other areas of your life spilling over into the mix. That's perfectly okay, our lives are not so separate that what happens at home doesn't affect how you feel at work and vice versa.

You may be surprised by what you feel or say. Chances are you've been bottling up stressful stuff for quite some time, and are finally getting it out. Keep writing until you feel you have exhausted the answers to your question (but hopefully not yourself).

Now if you like, read over what you've penned. Does anything surprise you? Do you see any patterns to situations, behaviors or people? Did you find any solutions or ideas that will help you in the future? Take a few minutes to glean what may be useful for you.

Next, crumble, fold, tear or cross out the writing, and making sure to have a non-flammable receptacle, set the paper on fire (I would not recommend this if you typed on your computer). As you watch it burn, mentally or verbally let go of all the feelings associated with what you've written. You held the stress in your body, writing it down moved it outside your body, and symbolically burning it will take it away.

If using a match inside is against the rules where you are, tearing or shredding the pages will also symbolize letting go of the stress. You will most likely feel freer than before, and perhaps even optimistic about the future.

Meditate-Breathe

Meditation is a practice of concentrated focus upon a sound, object, visualization, the breath, or movement, in order to increase awareness of the present moment, reduce stress, promote relaxation, and enhance personal and spiritual growth. Sounds like just what the doctor ordered. If you've never tried it, give it a few tries to notice the benefits. It gets easier and more enjoyable with practice.

The process is easy and painless, so sit back and enjoy! First, turn off or silence any possible distractions. Next, decide if you want to concentrate on your breathing, or repeating a word (such as Calm, Relax, or Om) either in your head or out loud. The idea is to focus on one of these two things instead of any other thoughts or distractions.

Set a timer, if necessary. Find a comfortable chair and sit with both feet planted firmly on the floor. Or sit on the floor with your legs comfortably crossed, knees out to the sides. Sit in a position that you feel you could hold for the duration of the meditation- in this case up to an hour.

Close your eyes and relax as much as you can.

Breathe deeply, paying attention to your inhale for four counts, and then out for four counts. If you plan to concentrate on your breath, continue to count it in and out. If you decide to focus on a word (mantra), repeat the word to yourself on every exhale.

As you go along, thoughts will come into your mind, try to let them go without much attention and continue with your attention to your breath or mantra. This will happen repeatedly, but just brush the intruding thoughts aside for now. Concentrate on breathing and you will find yourself relaxing more as time goes by.

When your timer rings, and your time for meditation is over, remain still until you feel ready to open your eyes.

Take a few minutes to jot down thoughts, feelings, or images you experienced during the session. This is a great habit to start after meditation, because you may have discovered solutions to problems, or creative insights to pursue later. You will feel more relaxed, and perhaps more clear-headed and energized. Whatever you now need to address may suddenly seem less an obstacle and more an interesting endeavor.

That's it! Easy, but very effective.

Yoga

Sometimes relaxing only requires stretching your muscles to release the pent up energy stored in them. When your muscles get so tense that they start sending you painful de-stress signals, one first line of defense is to stretch them out. Work out some of the lactic acid build-up and they will move more freely. If you have just a couple places you feel the stress, work specifically on those.

Yoga poses are amazing for stretching gently, and one overall fantastic stretching pose is a dead man pose. Lie on the floor on your back, legs and arms straight. Just relax each part of your body into the floor, muscle by muscle. Start at your feet and deliberately relax your feet, then your calves, thighs, and so on up to your head. As you pay attention to each body part, you will feel the release, until you just melt into the floor.

If you can't lie on the floor, another way to stretch your body is to stand with your feet shoulder width apart, and bend over at the waist until you feel the stretch in your back and legs. Let your head and arms dangle. Hold this and breathe deeply. As you relax and your muscles unkink, you will sink lower to the ground. Hold as long as is comfortable. Do this periodically throughout the day as you start to feel tense.

There are so many great videos for Yoga and Stretching. You can try some out on Netflix or Amazon Prime before buying ones that you enjoy. I have one video that has three ten minute yoga workouts, one for morning, one for evening and one specifically for stress reduction. They usually recommend using a yoga mat (so you don't slip in some of the poses), and sometimes a strap, but in a pinch you can use the carpet with bare feet and a towel. Quick, easy and very effective. You may use your hour with poses and end with the dead man pose to relax the rest of the time.

Om...

Soothing Bath

This is one of my favorite ways to relax and shut out the rest of the world. All you need is your favorite bath oil or bubbles, add some Epsom salts if you have sore muscles, and the warmest water you can stand.

Make sure the rest of your household knows you are unavailable for the duration. Place a DO NOT DISTURB sign on the bathroom door if that will help. Then add some of your favorite items for ambiance. Use candles, soft music, a glass of wine, your latest novel, or anything else you like.

This is not meant to be work, so just relax, let the water soak away your cares....

What cares?

Schedule Another Stress Tamer

If you've tried one of these Hour+ strategies, and still feel stressed, try another one, or do one a second time, as long as your time permits. A great pre-emptive strategy is to put a 30-60 minute block of Less-Stress time on your calendar every day to keep stress at bay. At the very least, incorporate a 5 minute tension-zapper every hour or two to insure you feel your best.

What do you have to lose? (How about some of that Stress you're feeling...) There's so much more to gain...

1 Hour At Work

At work, finding an hour may only be available at lunchtime. That's still perfect for blasting away at stress and its ill-effects on you. Find a way to be kind to yourself and your body/mind will surely thank you later. Onward, to a calmer place...your workmates will also thank you.

Eat Lunch Outside

Even when you don't have time to go out for lunch, you can still go outside for lunch. You may have limited options for nice spots to sit, but even so if you can take your food with you outdoors, you can at least get a change of scenery, and even better, get a chance to breathe in some relaxing fresh air.

If you are not someone who normally packs a lunch for work, perhaps you can order lunch delivered and still enjoy eating outside. It may be a great idea to try to keep your office fridge or desk drawer stocked with easy to carry food choices: yogurt, trail mix, protein bars, string cheese, fresh fruits and veggies. Then, when the mood strikes, you can easily take a break outside and get away.

This simple act can help you forget what is on your desk for a while, and give you some time to get some fresh air, people watch or just catch a few rays of vitamin D. A change of locale can be simple but effective at alleviating stress. It can also be a chance to enjoy time to clear your mind and nourish your body.

Make it a new appointment on your weekly calendar for continued relaxation.

And bonus, save some money (and calories) by not eating out!

Take a Walk

If you can get away from your office or desk for a while, but not leave the building, why not get some exercise to alleviate the tension? Walk around, say hi to some colleagues you don't often see, or do a few flights of stairs and get your heart pumping.

You could shake off the tired, frustrated, bored feeling and jump start the rest of your day. Sometimes I like to walk around even for ten or fifteen minutes and think about something I love, a favorite movie, person or food and my mood will shift immediately. Then, keep the refreshed feeling with you as you continue your day. Or, if needed, take a few more walks throughout your time at work, and stay more upbeat and energized.

Eat Some Comfort Food $

This one may require advance planning, unless you can run out to pick up some comfort food. The reason this helps cut down your stress level is because comfort foods provide you with just that-comfort. The foods you eat can take you to places in your past or with people who give you joy.

This can be a welcome relief when you are especially stressed with your day. Many comfort foods involve stick-to-your-ribs type meals, potatoes and meat, pasta dishes, ice cream or other dessert-fare. I wouldn't recommend using this solution frequently if your comfort food encourages additional pounds on your frame, but when you really need it, this can be a lifesaver.

Plan ahead, or find out the nearest place that has meatloaf and mashed potatoes, so you don't have to stress out trying to find it. Or, if comfort food is portable, like microwave buttered popcorn or chocolate, keep a supply in your desk.

But make it a treat, for when you really need it.

Enjoy!

Window Shop

This may not be an appealing option for everyone, but it can be a legitimate diversion from your day. The idea is to take your mind off of your stress, and do a little mindless daydreaming.

If you happen to find yourself near some shops, take a stroll and pause in front of the shop windows to get a good look at what the store is promoting. You may find some items which make you smile, or wonder who in the world would buy that, or find the perfect gift to get for Uncle Bill for his birthday. Make a note to purchase it later...

Spend a few minutes imagining yourself wearing that beautiful Rolex watch or cooking up some Creme Brulee with the portable torch. This activity is an escape, a chance to clear your mind of all that stresses you right now, and look at some fun stuff.

Just be sure to keep your shopping in your mind, for now, so as not to add more stress (unless finding something you need helps make your life easier, of course). Have some fun with it!

Write It Down & Tear It Up

This can be an extremely cathartic activity. If you are not one who generally likes to write, I encourage you to give it a try at least once. There is also the 'Tear It Up' part of the process you won't want to miss! (See also, Write it Down and Burn It activity in 1 Hour at Home)

Sometimes, if you haven't anyone nearby who will listen to you release your frustration, or the office walls will allow the words to seep outside your safe space, the next best thing is to write it down. And it may even become your preferred method.

Pull out some old fashioned paper and a pen. You can write using a computer keyboard, but it's much easier and more gratifying to use ink and flourishes to get out your anxiety.

~Stress-Less in 5 Minutes~

Take a minute or more to collect your thoughts, asking yourself, *"What is it that is bothering/frustrating/angering/stressing me?"* Let the question percolate for a bit, until you feel like writing down all that comes to mind.

This is not the time to hold back, just let everything you can think of flow through the pen to the paper. Nobody is going to see it. As you write, you may find other areas of your life spilling over into the mix, that's okay, our lives are not so separate that what happens at work doesn't affect how you feel at home and vice versa.

You may be surprised by what you feel or say. Chances are you've been bottling up stressful stuff for quite some time, and are finally getting it out. Keep writing until you feel you have exhausted the answers to your question (but hopefully not yourself).

Now if you like, read over what you've penned. Does anything surprise you? Do you see any patterns to situations, behaviors or people? Did you find any solutions or ideas that will help you in the future? Take a few minutes to glean what may be useful for you.

Next, crumble, fold, tear up or cross out the writing, (I would not recommend this if you typed on your computer) and making sure to really exaggerate making the pages no more than the smallest of scraps. Really get into it. This process can also let you get rid up pent-up energy. As you do this, mentally or verbally let go of all the feelings associated with what you've written. You held the stress in your body, writing it down moved it outside your body, and symbolically destroying it will take it away.

You will most likely feel a greater sense of freedom than before, and perhaps even optimistic about the future.

The future is a blank page...waiting for you...

Take a Cat Nap

I'm not entirely sure why they call a quick nap a 'cat nap', since I've been around cats all my life, and it seems to me that they can sleep indefinitely, and only wake up to the sound of food being opened, or to physical coaxing.

Regardless, when you have about 45 minutes, and you feel exhausted, it's the perfect time for a short, but extremely beneficial nap. To get the most benefit, find a comfortable spot, could be your favorite comfortable chair in the office, or you can roll out a blanket, yoga mat or towel on the floor.

Remove as many distractions as possible: perhaps lock the office door, turn off or silence phones, other gadgets, including streaming light on your face. I recently acquired a fantastic eye mask on a flight on Emirates Airlines and now find that I sleep much more soundly. Try this if you have trouble sleeping during the day. If you need to watch your time, set a timer or alarm for 45 minutes, and then let go.

If it helps, you can try to empty your mind, or tell yourself to relax, or sleep to encourage rest. Chances are, you'll fall asleep easily, and awaken more refreshed, and better able to handle the days' challenges.

Unless the cat woke you up early…

Listen to Calming/Happy Music

Music can have a profound effect on us. Hearing a certain song can take you back to a particular place and time, complete with all the feelings associated with that time.

This makes a perfect stress-buster, provided you have music which you know takes you to a positive place or invokes a feeling of peace, happiness and serenity. Try to find a few songs, or genres of music which take you to a happy place. If you don't have anything handy, try an online music program or radio station that plays your favorite tunes. If you need to use headphones, make sure you keep some nearby. Some people find instrumental or classical can be calming, even inspiring. Others enjoy coffeehouse, acoustic music. You may enjoy music which makes you want to dance around.

No worries, just turn it up and breathe in the joy!

Change Your Location

Sometimes at work the walls can seem as though they are closing in on you. Not helpful when you have serious demands on your time and energy. Take a short walk within the building to shake away the cobwebs of pent-up energy. If there are any spaces to get away to think-or work- go there to do some decompressing or perhaps some brainstorming. Possibilities include a break room, library, lobby, or even a window nook away from your office. Use a pad and pen to write down some ideas for your work or personal snags for fifteen minutes, or until you run out of ideas. Then go back to your office and work to implement the ones that make sense.

A change in location can push those walls back out and give you breathing room to get your work done more easily.

Shift Your Perspective

This one can be challenging, but ultimately can bring invaluable insights, new solutions, and even renewed excitement about your work. The idea is to look at your dilemma, whether with a person, a project or a situation, from another angle or perspective. It's a bit like the two heads are better than one concept, only you get to be both heads!

For a few minutes, try to put yourself in the shoes of another person who is part of your troubling circumstance. What do you think is their view of the situation? How do you think it affects them? What do you think they would consider a positive outcome?

Ponder these questions until you feel comfortable imagining their outlook on this. How does it help you see where you are in agreement? How can their needs or view help you to find more common ground? What can you do now that you hadn't considered before?

How do you feel about your next step? Chances are there is new hope, and new options to consider.

Way to go, now go get it done!

Ask For Help

This may seem like admitting defeat to some, but can actually be good for you and the person you ask for help. Chances are it will save you a good bit of time, and may even give someone else a needed challenge or distraction. Everyone needs help from time to time, but most don't feel comfortable asking for it. Since no man (or woman) is an island, it just makes sense to get some input from another member of your tribe to solve the problem in the best way possible.

Approach someone you trust and respect and ask if they can spare a few minutes to help you talk through your dilemma. Chances are they will be happy to help, maybe even feel great that they are needed. Bonus, you may actually enjoy the process, and have started a new trend of working together.

Let's do this!

Teach Someone Something

Take a moment to think about whether there is someone at work who you know is struggling with something with which you could help. They may or may not have asked for help, but you feel that you may be able to make their life easier. When you show another person how to do a new task, or learn a new skill, the gift you give them is forever theirs.

Approach them and offer your assistance or guidance in a way that is non-threatening. You've been there yourself, and wanted to make the task easier for them through your prior learning. You are offering yourself as a temporary mentor, and when you do help someone else to success, you feel pretty good as well.

And for a little while, you didn't think about your own stresses. With a new successful assist, you feel ready to take on your own challenges with a brighter perspective. You paid it forward, and you never know when it may come back to you.

Learn Something New

You know how people say, "You learn something new every day"? Well, the older you get, you may feel like this is not the case. As a kid, everything is new and interesting and offers learning opportunities. It is also said that elderly folks who challenge the mind stay the youngest and may keep senility at bay.

The one thing that learning new things offers everyone at any age is the brain focus required to really assimilate the process or information to fully learn it. You will be hard-pressed worrying about other things while trying to learn how to drive a manual transmission car.

If you need to do something drastic to change your head-space, how about spending an hour learning how to make a youtube channel. Or how to play bridge. Or cook a perfect omelette. Just find a book, or video that can show you the way, and really dive into learning. Take notes, or practice while you watch.

You'll soon forget what was keeping you so preoccupied. And you'll have a new skill to try out!

Win-Win!

List Your Accomplishments

This simple exercise can be so much fun, you may begin to wonder why you don't have your own jet to fly to your island paradise. Everyone has successes accumulated over time, and you may be surprised by all the simple ones you've forgotten. Here's your chance to brag about yourself, even if only on paper.

Pull out something to write on. Now take a few moments to journey back in time. Go all the way back to your first memories and stop on any that show you achieved something you set out to do-it doesn't matter the size or scope. If you won the spelling bee in second grade, write it down, preferably using difficult units of language (!).

Maybe you earned a 'best hitter' award, or put yourself through college working 2 jobs. Anything that you set out to do and accomplished is reason for celebration. You are a superhero. And when you finish writing down all you've done, you may feel more than ready to accept whatever challenge faces you now.

SuperYou...

List Your Skills

This is similar to listing your accomplishments, however, you may have skills you haven't thought about or used for a while. Maybe you have the ability for laser-focus to complete something important to you. If you haven't been participating in activities of import, you may not use this skill. But you have it, it's a part of you just waiting to be pulled out and put to good use.

Find something to write on, and label it *My (Amazing) SKILLS*.

Then think about the things you are good at. Add to the list what other people tell you that you are adept at (doesn't matter if you agree, just write it down). If you filled out the Accomplishments List (see previous activity), look at those and glean from them the skills you used so successfully.

Now you have a fantastic list of your strengths. Looking at them, is there anything you can't do? Are there any hidden skills you hadn't thought about that could help you out now? If a crucial skill is lacking, where can you go/what can you do to strengthen it? Or, who can you enlist to help you in this area?

You may be pleasantly surprised that you have most things covered. So, take a moment and appreciate all that you are and can do. Then, go ahead and flex some of those skill-muscles!

Schedule Another Stress Tamer

If you've tried one of these Hour+ strategies, and still feel stressed, try another one, or do one a second time, as long as time allows. A great pre-emptive strategy is to put a 30-60 minute block of Less-Stress time on your calendar every day to keep stress at bay. At the very least, incorporate a 5 minute tension-zapper every hour or two to insure you feel your best.

What do you have to lose? (Pain, unease, stuck-ness...) There's so much more to gain...

1 Hour Outside

If you are fortunate to have an hour and no place in particular to spend it, you have as many options as you can think of. Start with one of these tasks and find a place that you will get the most benefit out of completing it. Your choice can add to the stress-reducing results! Choose wisely...

Travel to the Stars $

Star-Gazing is one of the perfect ways to see the world, the universe as vast, making the worries of our lives seem much more insignificant. You can do this by lying down on a blanket outside (at night!), and just looking up. Notice any activity: constellations you recognize, planets that may be particularly bright, shooting stars, or even the blinking light of a 747.

Imagine yourself traveling through space, stopping to view earth from the North Star. If you can print one out before you go, take a map of the constellations to see how many you can find. You may also have the story behind the names. If you have a telescope, this will bring you closer to the action.

Of course, another option is to visit a planetarium, if you are lucky enough to live in a city (or the middle of nowhere) where there is one. Out in the middle of west Texas is the McDonald Observatory, and every night you can stand outside while a guide uses a laser pointer to highlight the view of the sky at that time. I've never seen so many stars! Indoors is also a great option, as most planetariums have amazing programs to get you into the feeling of the vastness of the universe.

It's a good thing to get a bit of perspective like this now and then. You just may look at the rest of your life a bit differently afterward. You will most likely feel more relaxed and awe-inspired.

Make star-gazing a habit to stay centered.

See Some Comedy $

Laughter is one of the best remedies for whatever ails you. Much research has been done on the benefits of belly laughs and the release of feel-good hormones, which can lessen stress-inducing hormones and reduce pain. Many physicians prescribe Laughter/Humor Therapy in addition to more traditional therapies for chronic pain or serious illness.

It can do wonders for relieving stress. It's even better when you go out with friends to see live comedy. Humor unites us, and is in fact contagious. To get the most belly laughs, do it with a roomful of people. Much comedy is based on the absurdity of everyday situations and experiences. Sometimes things we may think of as huge problems or obstacles can look different when a comic portrays these events as truly benign and laughable.

It's so true. Laugh until your belly (or your cheeks) hurts. Bonus- you're getting some great exercise.

Go to the Movies $

Want -or need- to escape your life altogether for a little while? What better way than to transport yourself into a different world, via a film? It's easy, it's available almost any time and you can do it alone without any problem. (Take a friend with you if you like, though!)

The key, of course is to find a movie that will take you away from your life without depressing you. Choose a genre you enjoy- comedy, sci-fi, dramedy, foreign (bonus, you have to totally concentrate if you need to read subtitles), chick flick , action, adventure, inspirational, animated... find one that sounds entertaining and go escape for a couple hours.

You may come out of it refreshed, inspired to tackle your life and perhaps with a creative purpose. That's why they keep making films, so we can continue to live vicariously through the characters.

You are the director of your own life, and you can rewrite it at any time. Flex those creative muscles and move forward in a positive way. You will feel better, guaranteed.

Take a Course $

One reason stress can get a stronghold in our lives is that we spend precious little time doing things which we enjoy. Activities that feed the mind, soul and creative self. One way to alleviate this stress, is to take a course, learn something new. When you sign up for a course, you are committing time over a period of sessions to concentrate and explore something which excites and challenges you.

Think for a moment about any skills or subjects that you've been wishing you had the time to learn. Always wanted to get certified in scuba diving? How about learn to speak Italian? Creative writing, ceramics, basic car maintenance, selling real estate, landscaping, creating apps for cell phones; you name it, there's probably a class (and an app!) that teaches how to do it.

And, you may not even have to go anywhere. Many colleges, community colleges and even cities have online courses you can work on at your own pace. You can still take a class that meets on campus or a community center or even the swimming pool, but wherever it is, you will be doing something strictly for you.

When you take care of you, you are better able to deal with stress when it pops up. If you go to class, you meet other people interested in the same topic or skill and may find new friends. Taking a course can be just for fun, but doubles as a proactive strategy to keep stress from taking over your life.

Who knows, you may even find your calling, or your next best thing.

Plan Your Dream Vacation

What better place to dream about your ultimate vacation than out in the fresh air? If you can, find a place to sit with a view that inspires you.

It could be a park, a plaza, your backyard, just somewhere that gets your creative ideas fueled. I tend to love sitting by water, as it soothes and mesmerizes me. Whatever works for you.

Have some paper, or in a pinch your electronic gadget. Do you have a bucket list of places you want to visit? Or just one trip that you've been thinking about for longer than you care to admit. That's perfect, start here. If not, take a few minutes and brainstorm some trips of a lifetime.

Now, pick one to plan. Make a list of the places you want to see, where you'd like to stay, how long the trip should be, passport-visa-immunizations, what time of year is best, how much to budget for transportation, lodging, meals, activities...

As you write down all the details you can think of to plan, you may find that more research is needed. That's great, you're one step closer to taking off on your vacation. Highlight what needs more information, and perhaps ideas about where to gather it- travel agency, city or country websites, friends who have travelled to your destination. You can even write out one or more possible itineraries. Really get into the plan, picture the trip in your mind. What do you see, smell, hear, taste, feel?

Now you can see this trip as a reality. Now you can put the plan into motion, and before you know it you'll be posting your pictures holding up the leaning tower of Pisa to friends.

And, by the way, don't you feel better? Excited, not stressed? Yeah, bon voyage!

Get a Massage $

Doesn't just the idea of a massage make you relax? I remember the first time I had one, I was tense, and for the first couple days afterward I felt extremely sore. I didn't think the whole massage thing was all it touted to be. But, I went again and had a much better experience, feeling wonderful, relaxed and energized at the same time.

Now I realize the value of taking the time to be good to my body. Yes, it costs time and money, but absolutely, you will feel better once the time spent working out the kinks (stress!) is finished.

Picture it in your mind...warm massage oil...soft music...pleasant fragrances...expert hands working on all the sore and knotted muscles...ahhh...make your appointment now.

Acupuncture $

If you've never heard of or tried acupuncture, it can seem very foreign to you. It is a far eastern tradition involving super-thin needles inserted into various areas of your body along what's known as meridians. It may even sound painful (it's really not), but thankfully has become more and more commonplace in most cities in the US.

Many places have low-cost, walk-in centers that provide you with a typically 1-1 ½ hour treatment based on your particular areas of pain or stress. Based on this consultation with the Acupuncturist, he will determine where to place the super-thin needles to treat your concerns. Treatment may concentrate on one or many issues, including pain, stress, stomach problems, headaches, weight loss, insomnia, anything you can imagine, really.

You then lie or sit in a lounging chair comfortably, usually in a darkened room, while the process does its work. You may even fall asleep (bonus for the sleep-deprived). Once he removes the super-thin needles, you leave feeling refreshed. If you haven't, but are open to trying something new, I highly recommend acupuncture.

Why not?

Visit a Friend

Time goes by quickly, and frequently this means that we don't have opportunities to see the people who mean the most to us as often as we'd like. Why not make today one of those times?

You know who the friends and family are that always bring a smile to your face, offer sage advice, or just plain help you forget the problems you face. Spend some time with one of them. He/she may just be needing your sage advice today, too.

Use your friend lifeline...

Read or Write

When you're stressed, a book can take you to another place, or invite you to look at things differently. You can read anything that you enjoy that won't make you feel more tense. But to really get yourself out of stress-mode, a book that will inspire you to think big, to consider that there is more to this life than surviving the daily grind.

If you're not sure what to read, try searching at a library, bookstore or online for Inspirational or Motivational books. They may not be the 'can't put it down until I'm finished' kind of reading, but if you spend an hour with a good uplifting book, you will feel better, and may even have ideas about how to improve your situation.

I imagine you'll even smile once or twice. Try it. And carry the book with you, leave it in the car or your office, for whenever you need a pick-me-up -motivationally.

I try not to leave home without something to read. It's easier since the invention of electronic readers, tablets and even smart phones, but I also enjoy the feel of the pages in an old-fashioned book.

The key for this activity is to read something that will somehow calm you down. Whether you pick a book that inspires, makes you laugh or engrosses you in solving a mystery, the beauty of reading is that it transports you away from your present place with all that comes with it, to another, different place where you can laugh, slay dragons or fall in love.

The same idea applies to writing. If you have a journal, or are working on your novel, being outside can be inspirational to the writing process. Have a notebook or pad of paper with you, like a book, and you'll always have something to do. Write without rules, just let the words flow out, stream of consciousness-like onto the page. It's also pretty cathartic.

Guaranteed to rewrite your current stress.

Don't leave home without them.

Take a Hike

Walking is just about the best exercise available. Not that long ago, it wasn't even considered exercise, it was just what you did to get around. Of course that was before we could drive everywhere, even buy food, do the banking and wash the car, without ever having to step out of the vehicle. Now, unless you live in Downtown, Large City, Anywhere, chances are you don't have to walk that much during the day. So, we strap on pedometers and fancy fitness bracelets and attempt to recreate the type of walking we used to do naturally.

Hiking is walking, but generally on a scenic route, perhaps with variable terrain and best done with the appropriate boots/shoes and if you like, a cool walking stick. When you want to be outside, why not take advantage of the many vistas available when you walk a park trail? You will soak up some Vitamin D, see some interesting flora and fauna and perhaps even meet your daily pedometer goal. Oh, and you'll also feel better. With each step, let go of the stress and soak in the fresh air. You may lose track of time, but not the benefits of the hike!

Window Shop

This may not be an appealing option for everyone, but it can be a legitimate diversion from your day. The idea is to take your mind off of your stress, and do a little mindless daydreaming.

If you happen to be near some shops, take a stroll and pause in front of the shop windows to get a good look at what the store is promoting. You may find some items which make you smile, or wonder who in the world would buy that, or find the perfect gift to get for Uncle Bill for his birthday. Take a picture of the gift or make a note to purchase it later...

Spend a few minutes imagining yourself wearing that beautiful Rolex watch or cooking up some Creme Brulee with the portable torch, and again, this activity is an escape, a chance to clear your mind of your life stress and instead look at some fun stuff.

Just be sure to keep your shopping in your mind, for now (unless making the purchase alleviates some stress!). Have some fun with it!

Enjoy a Hobby $

If you have a favorite hobby, but can't remember the last time you took time to enjoy it, now might be the perfect time to dust it off and indulge. If it's been a very long time, just to refresh your memory, a hobby is an activity which while nobody is requiring or paying you to participate, you are completely lost in time while you are doing it.

Examples might be a sport, a club, assembling a collection, an artistic endeavor, learning a language or anything else you can get lost in while pursuing. You can do it alone or with a group. The key is to take some time to do something you love.

Once you do, you'll wonder why you ever stopped, and will most likely find it easier to schedule your hobby into your life again. Take the feeling with you.

~1 Hour Outside~

Go to the Beach

If you are lucky enough to live near an ocean, the beach is a fantastic place to let go of some stress. No matter the season, the beach offers the same rolling waves and cacophony of seagulls to lull you into a less frenetic space.

Sit, stand walk or even run along the shore or in the surf. Find a comfortable spot and drink in the sounds, smells, sights and feel of all that's around you. Concentrate on what's going on outside and you won't pay attention to what you're feeling inside. Explore the area for interesting shells, rocks or people.

Whatever you find at the beach, let it help you see the big picture of life, and not dwell so much on the smaller troubles. You can handle those now.

Visit a Museum $

Another great way to transport yourself to another time or place is to visit a local museum. Take yourself back in time at a Natural History museum, or explore the world through art, local history or science. Maybe you prefer a hands-on museum, such as a pioneer town or space museum where you can experience what life was like for those who were there.

The idea is to get out of your present and spend a bit of time elsewhere. You may even learn something new, or go to a museum that you've driven by countless times but never before visited. Much like the visit to an observatory, this may help you see more of the big picture of life, and not dwell as much on what's really not that important, or as bad as you think.

A new perspective can do wonders. Time well spent, don't you think?

Go to the Library or a Book Store $

A great place to help you leave the realm of stress is the library. Just walking through the aisles of books, movies, and music can bring your imagination to life. You may have a topic you've been meaning to learn more about, or just wander until something catches your eye.

I find that when I do this, I'm reminded that I want to look into finding a class to learn sign language, or travel information on Switzerland, or even how much the trade-in value of my car is right now. The possibilities are endless. The same is true for a bookstore. You can find a few books to browse and find a cozy chair to fill the time.

Anything that requires your attention is going to encourage your mind to follow a different path, away from the problems you face. Or, you may find in the pages ideas which can help you solve the problem.

Either way, you can be stress-free while buried in the world of words.

Schedule Another Stress Tamer

If you've tried one of these Hour+ strategies, and still feel stressed, try another one, or do one a second time, as long as time allows. A great pre-emptive strategy is to put a 30-60 minute block of Less-Stress time on your calendar every day to keep stress at bay. At the very least, incorporate a 5 minute tension-zapper every hour or two to insure you feel your best.

What do you have to lose? (Pain, worry, ...) There's so much more to gain...

5. De-Stress Quotes!

When you just need a pick-me-up to move forward, here is a collection of quotes specifically related to stress and how to alleviate it. I hope you find inspiration and relief in them. Feel free to print them out, or choose your favorites to attach to your computer, fridge or mirror!

To your BEST Life!

"The greatest weapon against stress is our ability to choose one thought over another."

William James

~~~~~

"It's not stress that kills us, it is our reaction to it."

Hans Selye

~~~~~

"We must have a pie. Stress cannot exist in the presence of a pie."

David Mamet

~~~~~

"If you want to conquer the anxiety of life, live in the moment, live in the breath."

Amit Ray

~~~~~

"My body needs laughter as much as it needs tears. Both are cleansers of stress."

Mahogany Silver Rain

~~~~~

"The only difference between a rut and a grave are the dimensions."

Ellen Glasgow

~~~~~

"Come back!" the Caterpillar called after her. "I've something important to say."

This sounded promising, certainly. Alice turned and came back again.

"Keep your temper," said the Caterpillar."

Lewis Carroll, Alice's Adventures in Wonderland

~~~~~

"Stress is the trash of modern life-we all generate it but if you don't dispose of it properly, it will pile up and overtake your life."

Danzae Pace

~De-Stress Quotes~

~~~~~

"Never hurry and never worry. -Charlotte"

— E.B. White, Charlotte's Web

~~~~~

"When I take a break, even just a brief one, the creative energy flows in. Only then do I have anything of value to share with others. Once I recognized this, I stopped feeling guilty about taking time for myself."

Holly Mosier

~~~~~

"I'm going to tell you a secret:

You don't have to believe every thought that pops into your head."

B. Dave Walters

~~~~~

"Letting go is the willingness to change your beliefs in order to bring more peace and joy into your life instead of holding onto beliefs that bring pain and suffering..."

Hal Tipper

~~~~~

"Sometimes a pat on the back or just a simple word of comfort is all that it takes to bring someone under heavy stress back to balance."

JA Perez

~~~~~

"My doctor told me to avoid unnecessary stress, so I stopped going to doctors."

Shira Tamir

~~~~~

"If you're stressing over happiness, you're doing it wrong!"

Shannon L. Alder

~~~~~

"At some point, I finally realized that stress made a really bad companion... so I had it pack its shit and leave."

Steve Maraboli

~~~~~

"No matter how much you stress or obsess about the past or future, you can't change either one. In the present is where your power lies."

Mandy Hale

~~~~~

"If you keep running into the same wall over and over again, turn."

Crystal DeLarm Clymer

~~~~~

~De-Stress Quotes~

"Behind every stressful thought is the desire for things to be other than they are."

Toni Bernhard

~~~~~

"There are often great lessons to be learned at the roots of stress, drama, and heartache. Don't let the magnitude of the circumstance blind you to the value of the lesson."

Steve Maraboli

~~~~~

"Stop stressin' and be a blessin'."

T.F. Hodge

~~~~~

"Peace of mind arrives the moment you come to peace with the contents of your mind."

Rasheed Ogunlaru

~~~~~

"At any time, you can rethink your life and reinvent yourself. "

"Choose your words better and say/affirm exclusively what you aspire to create in your life."

"Dare to dream and dare to stand out. Get off the beaten path."

Denise Pitre

~~~~~

~Stress-Less in 5 Minutes~

"When in doubt, do something that makes you feel better, you deserve to be happy."

Tyra LaRocca

~~~~~

About Tyra LaRocca

After years working as a College Counselor, Mom to three, successful entrepreneur and shoe saleswoman extraordinaire, she decided to put her energy into writing, coaching and training people like herself to figure out how to make the most of this short, but oh-so-sweet time on earth. As a result, you may find her attempting to converse in another language in a foreign land, or in Austin, Texas, where there is always something new and funny to experience or commit to writing. She believes that everyone has an interesting life story. Even you.

Especially YOU...Carpe Diem.

Thanks for Spending Your Precious Time with Me!

I would love to hear your thoughts or your own favorite stress-busting tips. Email me at Tyra@outsidetheboxlifecoach.com. You can also sign up for my newsletter at http://OutsideTheBoxLifeCoach.com for weekly stress and happiness tips. When you do you'll receive a FREE Happiness Quotes ebook as my gift!

You can also check for updates and join discussions about the book, or banishing stress at the website for the book: http://StressLessin5Minutes.com

If you found anything in this book which inspired, helped, or gave you hope, I'd so appreciate a review of this book on Amazon at http://www.amazon.com/dp/B015UK1DTG (Copy and paste this link)

Thank you in advance, you are amazing!

You May Also Like...

My other book, The Funny Thing About Happiness. This is my first book, available on Amazon. (http://www.amazon.com/dp/B00HYOAWT4)

Here's a peak at it:

Do you wonder why happiness seems so fleeting? Or how to find ways to be happier whenever you want? How about looking at the world in a new way while having some fun finding your way to happiness?

How could a Time Travel Watch help you be happier? How about a Portable Pause Button, allowing you to pause real life? Or a Magic-Wave, which cooks anything in any quantity at the touch of a button?

Awaken your imagination, and follow me on a journey to more happiness here...

Reader Reviews:

"Easy fast read! It had plenty of a-ha moments in it for me. This would be the perfect gift for someone you know that is simply down in the dumps. After reading it you will feel gratitude, freedom, and in control of your own happiness. I want my husband and kids to read it too. Thank you!" - Kristie J.

"This was such a fun book to read and really made me feel good after reading it! It really gave me a positive and new perspective on life. In addition, not only did it give me new ideas/tools to apply to my life it made me laugh which is always a plus! "- Taryn I.

Happiness Quotes, is a free book of quotes and comments to inspire you to smile and enjoy life. It's available Free when you sign up for my Newsletter as my gift to you.

~Extras~

Want More Personal Attention?

Life Coaching May Be Perfect For You!

If you feel like you need more ideas and accountability to meet your personal life or career goals, I can Help you! Life coaching is the perfect way to have a concerned but unbiased sounding board, partner in success and generally fun and productive coach for your goal achievement.

Find out more about Life Coaching Benefits and check out my programs, available in person (Austin, TX area) or by Skype/Phone.

Available are 1-1 Coaching , Group Coaching and Coaching Courses to work at your own pace.

If you have more questions, check out the FAQ's at http://OutsideTheBoxLifeCoach.com/get-coached or email me at Tyra@outsidetheboxlifecoach.com.

Let's discuss how we can work together to get you living your best life.

I also offer Courses on Udemy.com which allow you to study a topic at your own pace. Help and feedback is available as part of the program.

Be Happier NOW! This course is all about helping you see what your happy life would look and feel like for YOU. It is about learning and incorporating into your life every day simple steps that will infuse it with joy.

Happiness is yours to have and experience at any time. It doesn't require spending too much money or time for precious little joy. You just bring your willingness to look at your life objectively, and to do something every day that makes you happy.

In the works is a course called, *When You Reach Rock Bottom, Take a Climbing Course.* All about getting out of your rut, and into your best life. Check Udemy.com or follow my website for updates on when it will be available!

Thank you again for your time. I dearly hope you find the tools here to help you feel better, less stressed, about your daily life. I wish you only the best, and perhaps we'll meet someday along lifes' road.

Until then, BE AMAZING!

19650176R00063

Printed in Great Britain
by Amazon